SKATEBOARDING

Greenwood Guides to Extreme Sports

Surfing: The Ultimate Guide
Douglas Booth

Snowboarding: The Ultimate Guide
Holly Thorpe

BASE Jumping: The Ultimate Guide
Jason Laurendeau

Rock Climbing: The Ultimate Guide
Victoria Robinson

SKATEBOARDING
The Ultimate Guide

Becky Beal

GREENWOOD GUIDES TO EXTREME SPORTS
Holly Thorpe and Douglas Booth, Series Editors

 GREENWOOD

AN IMPRINT OF ABC-CLIO, LLC
Santa Barbara, California • Denver, Colorado • Oxford, England

Library of Congress Cataloging-in-Publication Data

Beal, Becky.
  Skateboarding : the ultimate guide / Becky Beal.
    p. cm. — (Greenwood guides to extreme sports)
  Includes bibliographical references and index.
    ISBN 978–0–313–38112–6 (cloth : alk. paper) — ISBN 978–0–313–38113–3 (ebook)
1. Skateboarding. I. Title.
GV859.8.B4   2013
796.22—dc23   2012035631

ISBN: 978–0–313–38112–6
EISBN: 978–0–313–38113–3

17 16 15 14 13   1 2 3 4 5

This book is also available on the World Wide Web as an eBook.
Visit www.abc-clio.com for details.

Greenwood
An Imprint of ABC-CLIO, LLC

ABC-CLIO, LLC
130 Cremona Drive, P.O. Box 1911
Santa Barbara, California 93116-1911

This book is printed on acid-free paper ∞

Manufactured in the United States of America

To Jennifer Sexton, my best friend and partner

contents

Series Foreword, ix

Preface, xi

Acknowledgments, xiii

Skateboarding Timeline, xv

1. Introduction: Alternative and Mainstream, 1

2. Origins and Development of Skateboarding, 7

3. Venues for Creativity: Sites, Events, and Competitions, 43

4. Pioneers and Heroes, 61

5. Navigating the Built Environment: Technology and Physics, 91

6. Future Trends, 103

Resource Guide, 109

Glossary, 119

Bibliography, 125

Index, 137

series foreword

of interest to students and enthusiasts alike, extreme sports are recharging and redefining athletics around the world. While baseball, soccer, and other conventional sports typically involve teams, coaches, and an extensive set of rules, extreme sports more often place the individual in competition against nature, other persons, and himself or herself. Extreme sports have fewer rules, and coaches are less prominent. These activities are often considered to be more dangerous than conventional sports, and that element of risk adds to their appeal. They are at the cutting edge of sports and are evolving in exciting ways.

While extreme sports are fascinating in their own right, they are also a window on popular culture and contemporary social issues. Extreme sports appeal most to the young, who have the energy and daring to take part in them, and who find in them an alternative culture with its own values and vocabulary. At the same time, surfing and various other extreme sports have long histories and are important to traditional cultures around the world. The extreme versions of these sports sometimes employ enhanced technology or take place under excessively challenging conditions. Thus they build on tradition yet depart from it. Extreme sports are increasingly significant to the media, and corporations recognize the marketing value of sponsoring them. Thus extreme sports become linked with products, their star athletes become celebrities, and their fans are exposed to a range of media messages. Local governments might try to regulate skateboarding and other extreme activities, sometimes out of safety concerns and sometimes out of moral ones. Yet other communities provide funding for skateboard parks, indoor rock climbing facilities, and other venues for extreme sports enthusiasts. Thus extreme sports become part of civil discourse.

Designed for students and general readers, this series of reference books maps the world of extreme sports. Each volume looks at a particular sport and includes information about the sport's history, equipment and techniques, and important players. Volumes are written by professors or other authorities and are informative, entertaining, and engaging. Students using these books learn about sports that interest them and discover more about cultures, history, social issues, and trends. In doing so, they become better prepared to engage in critical assessments of extreme sports in particular and of society in general.

Holly Thorpe and Douglas Booth, Series Editors

preface

i started taking skateboarding seriously in the summer of 1989. I was a graduate student studying the sociology of sport when I came across a group of skateboarders who sparked my imagination and with whom I shared a similar set of values. I ended up writing my dissertation on the social worlds of skateboarders. Ever since, much of my academic research has focused on the cultural dynamics of skateboarding. Twenty-three years later, I am still engrossed in a sport that has simultaneously changed and yet stayed the same.

The ethos of skateboarding resonates with me. It's fundamentally democratic: the participants are responsible for their own growth and development as well as the development of their friends' skill sets and the activity itself. Most skaters do not rely on coaches or a rule book; instead, skateboarders are the ones who construct the activity. It's fundamentally artistic: the goal of skateboarding is to create innovative ways of moving oneself and the board through space. Skateboarders are keenly aware of rhythms, tempos, and flows while navigating different spaces. These experiences alter one's sense of self and through them, one creates a unique style. Skateboarding encourages individual interpretation and expression. Style matters.

This book is a tribute to skateboarding. One that acknowledges that it is far from a perfect sport; some groups of people have benefited much more than others from it. Additionally, there are many social forces that work against its democratic and artistic impulses. This book invites you to examine the history and culture of skateboarding so that you can use the information provided to ask critical questions about who controls skateboarding and who benefits from skateboarding as a means to envision a more humane and just physical activity.

acknowledgments

through this project i have met many passionate, generous, and dedicated people and am very grateful for their support and encouragement. Special thanks to Patty Segovia-Krause, who gave much time and energy by providing photographs, information, feedback, and professional contacts. Another special thanks to Mike Horelick, who also provided information and continuous feedback. With respect to the technology and physics chapter, I am indebted to Paul Schmitt, Mike Rafter, Conley Reed, and James Hetrick for their contributions. Thanks to Bobby Smith for contributing photographs from the 1970s, to Elizabeth Gordon for her professional contacts in the field, and to Julien Laurent for his feedback and international perspective. I appreciate the institutional support from California State University–East Bay and the Department of Kinesiology. Thank you to Liem Tran for his work on the index. Finally, I want to thank editors Holly Thorpe, Doug Booth, George Butler, and Erin Ryan for their patience, support, and insightful guidance.

skateboarding timeline

1963

Larry Stevenson creates Makaha skateboards.

First organized skateboard contest is held in Hermosa Beach, CA. Sponsored by Makaha.

1964

Hobie Alter establishes the Hobie Skateboard brand.

Larry Gordon creates the FibreFlex skateboard.

1965

Quarterly Skateboarder is published, but only four issues.

ABC's *Wide World of Sports* covers the National Skateboard Championships in Anaheim, CA.

Pattie McGee, national girls' skateboard champion, is featured on the cover of *Life* magazine.

Skater Dater, a short film about a young male skater who deals with peer pressure, is made. Wins best short at Cannes Film Festival in 1966.

1966

The Devil's Toy, a short film based in Montreal that depicts skaters as rebellious and fighting against police, is made.

1968

Skip Engblom and Jeff Ho establish Zephyr Surfboards in Santa Monica, CA. It's the future sponsor of the renowned 1970s skateboarding team Z-Boys.

Skateboarding goes through a slump and isn't revitalized until the early 1970s.

1972

Frank Nasworthy develops the urethane wheel, replacing the clay wheels of the previous generation. He starts the company Cadillac Wheels.

1975

Skateboarder magazine is issued as a bimonthly. James O'Mahoney is the publisher, and Warren Bolster is editor and photographer.

Signal Hill (CA) Downhill contest begins. Guy Grundy wins going 50 miles per hour.

The Z-Boys make their presence known to the skateboarding community through their innovative styles during the Bahne-Cadillac National Championships at Del Mar (CA).

The Soul Artists of Zoo York crew is going strong and includes skateboarder Andy Kessler and graffiti artist Futura 2000.

1976

First formal skateboard park in United States opens in Port Orange, FL. Weeks later, the second park opens in Carlsbad, CA. By the late 1970s, there are close to 200 parks in the United States.

1977

Canadian Pro-Am Skateboarding Association is formed. Monty Little is the first president of the organization.

Pepsi sponsors a skateboarding team that includes Stacy Peralta and Russ Howell. Peralta and Howell tour Australia to promote skateboarding.

1978

Alan Gelfand is credited with inventing the ollie, a trick that would revolutionize skateboarding in the future.

The theatrical production *Skateboard Mania* featuring skaters Tony Jetton and Vickie Vickers opens.

Cal Jam II music festival with 300,000 in attendance conducts a skateboard exhibition that includes skaters Lauren Thornhill and Type Page.

Skateboard Kings, a documentary produced for BBC television, describes the skateboarding scene in Los Angeles.

Tony Alva, one of the original Z-Boys and top-rated skater, is featured in the movie *Skateboard*, which stars Leif Garrett.

First European Open held in Germany.

1979
Freestyler Russ Howell performs 163 continuous 360 spins, setting the record.

1980
Skateboarding is losing popular appeal as indicated by *Skateboarder* magazine, changing its format and name (*Action Now*) to include more sports.

California Amateur Skateboard League is created by Frank Hawk, Tony's father.

1981
Thrasher is established by Fausto Vitello.

1983
Transworld Skateboarding is established by Larry Balma.

National Skateboarding Association is created by Frank Hawk. Don and Daniel Bostick run the organization.

1984
Powell Peralta premieres its first video featuring its team, the Bones Brigade, produced by Stacy Peralta and Craig Stecyk.

1985
Tony Hawk and Christian Hosoi, two of the best vert skaters, face off in the Del Mar competition, initiating a celebrated rivalry throughout the 1980s.

1986
European Cup is held in Munster, Germany.

The skate competition held in Vancouver, B.C., during the World Exposition has been marked as the first truly international skateboarding competition.

1987
The Powell Peralta video *Search for Animal Chin* is released, creating the standard for skateboard videos.

1989

Munster Germany hosts a world cup competition.

Gleaming the Cube, a movie about a skateboarder, stars Christian Slater and includes skateboarders Tony Hawk and Mark Rogowski.

1990

Skateboarding goes through another lull as the recession of the early 1990s takes its toll. It's not until the exposure given to the sport through the X Games that its popularity booms again.

1992

Big Brother magazine is established by Steve Rocco. It is known for its sophomoric humor, explicit language and images, and is ultimately sold to Larry Flint Publications in 1997.

1993

Tampa Am competition series begins.

1994

World Cup Skateboarding is established by Don and Daniel Bostick.

Tampa Pro competition series begins.

1995

ESPN creates the Extreme Games (later called the X Games) and catapults skateboarding into the mainstream.

The International Association of Skateboard Companies is founded and led by Jim Fitzpatrick.

1996

The International Gravity Sports Association is formed by Marcus Rietema as the governing body for luge and downhill skateboarding.

1997

Patty Segovia-Krause establishes the All Girl Skate Jam (AGSJ), which becomes part of the Van's Warped tour in 2006.

1998

X Games expands globally and sponsors the Asia X Games.

1999
Tony Hawk is the first person to successfully land a 900, completed at the X Games in San Francisco.

Tony Hawk video game debuts, becoming one of the most successful video games throughout the next decade.

NBC establishes the Gravity Games competition series. It ends in 2006.

2001
Dogtown and Z-Boys, a critically acclaimed documentary produced by Stacy Peralta about the 1970s skating crew called Z-Boys, is released.

2002
Male skateboarders organize under the leadership of Andy MacDonald, creating the United Skateboarders Professional Association.

2003
Go Skateboarding Day is established by the International Association of Skateboarding Companies. It is celebrated every June 21.

2005
Female skateboarders organize under the leadership of Cara-Beth Burnside to form the Action Sports Alliance.

Tha Hood Games, a skate/art festival dedicated to inner-city neighborhoods, is established by Karl Watson and Keith Williams.

The Dew Tour competition series is established.

2006
Warren Bolster, famed skateboard photographer, dies.

Andy Kessler, original member of the Soul Artists of Zoo York, dies.

Fausto Vitello, the publisher of *Thrasher*, dies.

2007
Jake Brown falls nearly 45 feet while competing in the Big Air competition at the X Games. Luckily, he survived and is still skating.

Paranoid Park, a movie about teenage skaters in Portland, OR, is released.

2008
The Maloof Money Cup competition series is established, providing the biggest financial payout to date.

2009
Lyn-Z Adams Hawkins is the first female to land a 540 McTwist. She does this at the Quiksilver Tony Hawk show at the Grand Palais in Paris, France.

International Skateboarding Hall of Fame is established. First inductees include Tony Alva, Bruce Logan, Tony Hawk, and Danny Way. The following year, Bob Burnquist, Steve Cabellero, Torger Johnson, Eric Koston, Patti McGee, and Stacy Peralta are inducted.

2010
Rob Dyrdek forms The Street League competition series.

X Games Europe is established.

Over 2,000 skate parks are in operation in the United States.

Skateboarding industry is worth an estimated $4.5 to $5 billion.

1. introduction: alternative and mainstream

skateboarding has been touted as both an alternative and mainstream sport. Unlike football or hockey, skateboarding does not have formal rules or a standardized venue. It can be performed in a variety of ways and in virtually any space that has pavement. Although there are some formal competitions such as the X Games, skateboarding is regularly practiced as a more individualistic, creative, and process-oriented activity. Because of this orientation, skill and innovation are more valued than winning. It is not referees who judge skill, but other participants. Fundamentally, skateboarding is participant-run; it thrives on a do-it-yourself (DIY) ethos (Atencio & Beal, 2011; Borden, 2001; Chivers Yochim, 2010). Literally millions of people have taught themselves or relied on friends to learn how to ride a board and do tricks.

The everyday practice of skateboarding may be different from more traditional sports, but skateboarding is clearly part of mainstream society. Skateboarding is growing faster than any other sport in the United States. In 1998, 5.8 million people were skating and in 2007, there were 10.1 million participants. This represents a 74-percent growth rate, with the 12- to 17-year-olds generating most of this increase ("Skateboarding 10-year winner," 2008; Verdon, 2009). Current estimates range from 9 to 12 million participants in the United States (Montgomery, 2009; "Why Are Skateparks Beneficial," n.d.). To meet, and encourage, this demand, skate parks have been built in municipalities using both public and private funds. In the early 1990s, there were fewer than 200 skate parks in the United States; today, there are over 2,000 (Howell, 2008). The popularity of skateboarding is also evident in who young adults see as their role models. In 2008, Tony Hawk, the public face of skateboarding, was rated the top athlete, surpassing more traditional-sport athletes such as baseball player Derek Jeter and basketball player LeBron James (Badenhausen, 2009). The popularity of skateboarding can also be identified by its fiscal value. In the late 2000s, the global

1

skateboarding industry had an estimated worth between \$4.9 and \$5.5 billion (Glader, 2007; Howell, 2008). Additionally, top athletes are attractive to mainstream corporate sponsorship. Tony Hawk, who officially retired from professional skateboarding in 1999, earned \$12 million in 2008 from his sponsors, traveling road shows, and top-rated video games (Badenhausen, 2009).

Skateboarding has a global presence. There are national skateboarding governing bodies in most European countries and other countries such as Canada, Australia, and Brazil. In 2008, China invested US\$12 million to build a three-acre state-of-the-art skateboard and BMX park in Shanghai, which now is the site of the Asian X Games (Higgins, 2010, May 26, 2010). There have been many reports that the International Olympic Committee would like to introduce skateboarding to the Games, especially given the popularity of the recently added snowboarding events (Higgins, June 14, 2007; Thorpe & Wheaton, 2011). In 2007, two skaters from Australia started a skateboarding school in Kabul, Afghanistan, called Skateistan. The informal education has become a permanent skate park and school where participation by young boys and girls is blossoming, and has captured the attention of skaters across the globe who are volunteering their time and supplies. Plans are being made to build a similar school in Phnom Penh, Cambodia (Ellick, 2009; "Our story," n.d.). Similar efforts to use skateboarding as an outreach to disenfranchised youth are happening in Durban, South Africa (Wheaton, forthcoming). Skateboarding is also being used to promote tourism. For example, the Cayman Islands host the world's largest skate park, Black Pearl, at 62,000 square feet, which was built not to meet the local demand, but to encourage international travel for skaters and the industry.

Skateboarding has made its mark on popular culture as well. MTV has found that using skateboarders in their programs has proven successful. Their line-up of skateboarding-inspired shows has included *Viva La Bam, Jackass, Rob and Big, Rob Dyrdek's Fantasy Factory*, and *Life of Ryan*. MTV also featured several skateboarders on their show *Cribs*. *Jackass* was spun off to create three lucrative feature-length films. Skateboarding is also the topic of popular songs such as Avril Lavigne's 2002 hit "sk8er boi" and Lupe Fiasco's 2006 hit, "Kick, Push." Bart Simpson, the lead character of the longest running situation comedy (sit com) in the United States (started in 1989), *The Simpsons*, is often shown skateboarding, and Tony Hawk was a featured character in one of the shows. Additionally, skateboarding has influenced fashion trends, and "retailers that sell merchandise and clothing tied to skateboarding and snowboarding have become mall mainstays" (Verdon, 2009, para 2). As journalist Karl Greenfeld noted, "Skateboarding, second perhaps only to hip-hop, was the greatest influence on American youth culture of the late 20th century" (2004, 70).

With its growing popularity, people have created forms of skateboarding that move it closer to the traditional more bureaucratic forms of sport. For example, in the United States, Skate Pass is a popular curriculum that incorporates skateboarding with traditional physical education classes, and in California, there is an interscholastic skateboard league (Higgins, June 6 2007). Organizations like Drop into Skateboarding are promoting strategies to incorporate skateboarding into public recreation and schools facilities. The professionalization of competition, including the X Games, Street League, and the Maloof Money Cup, are structured in such a way that standards for the sport are regulated. With the heightened attention on professional competition, schools and camps populated by expert coaches who train eager skateboarders, such as Woodward Camps, have become more popular. This widespread acceptance and professionalization may seem odd to those who knew the days when skateboarders were assumed to be delinquent youth and skateboarding was an illegal activity in many cities (Howell, 2003).

why so popular now?

The dynamic interplay among the skateboarding industry, the youth market, general economic conditions, and mainstream media coverage have played a major role in the current degree of acceptance of skateboarding and skateboarders. The youth market has always been the target audience for skateboarding, but it was not until the 1980s that the industry intentionally distinguished itself from surfing (see the next chapter for more details), creating an identity that highlighted skateboarders as rebellious, cool, and street savvy. To maximize appeal for a youthful market, the industry promoted a whole lifestyle around skateboarding that included music, art, and fashion. In the 1990s, the millennial generation (people born between 1978 and 1995) was the most highly sought after market due to its numbers and wealth, and the highly "packaged" skateboarding lifestyle was a perfect avenue for mainstream commercial interests to reach this audience (Browne, 2004; Chivers Yochim, 2010; Kellet & Russell, 2009). During this period, the wealth and reach of such corporations as ESPN and the X Games, Mountain Dew, Nike, NBC, Adidas, and McDonalds entered

A skateboarder performs during an exhibition show at the Grand Palais in Paris, November 20, 2009. (AP Photo/Francois Mori)

the scene. Skateboarding and other "action," or "extreme," sports became the marker of the cool, independent teen. By the early 2000s, there were 1,141 registered trademarked products with *extreme* in their name (Browne, 2004). Additionally, skateboarding's D.I.Y. ethos and emphasis on creativity and innovation struck a chord with an audience whose identity is not primarily about skateboarding, but who supports the tenets of entrepreneurialism (Atencio & Beal, 2011; Heywood, 2006; Howell, 2005). For example, a National Public Radio (NPR) program in San Francisco, California, recently did a feature on Tommy Guerrero, who was a famous skateboarder during the 1980s. This program choice by NPR demonstrates that skateboarders and what they represent have a broad appeal. First, NPR's audience tends to be much older than the average skateboarder. Second, Guerrero was celebrated for attributes not directly associated with skateboarding but with traditional American values such as being a self-made man, an entrepreneur, and outstanding citizen: "We'll talk to Guerrero about his journey from high school dropout and teen skate god to entrepreneur and indie music icon. He joins us as part of our 'First Person' series featuring the leaders, innovators and other individuals who make the bay area unique" (Krasny, 2011).

This mainstream acceptance does not mean that there is consensus and harmony among the stakeholders. In fact, mainstream acceptance increases the number of interested parties who, in turn, have differing agendas for the sport. Struggles over the direction skateboarding should take, who should control skateboarding, and who should benefit from it continue. This book contextualizes the dynamic growth of skateboarding by addressing its history, culture, technology, and key participants. Although each chapter can be read for its own sake, they complement each other. Therefore, reading the whole book will provide a more robust picture. Nonetheless, it is not the intention to cover every fact or person, but to provide an overview of the major trends in order to shed some light on the factors and people that contribute to the cultural significance of skateboarding.

2. origins and development of skateboarding

tony hawk is one of the most well-known athletes in the United States. Rob Dyrdek and Ryan Scheckler have had successful television programs on MTV. *Dogtown and Z-Boys*, a recent documentary about skateboarding, won critical acclaim. Using a large ramp and his skateboard, Danny Way jumped the Great Wall of China. Currently skateboarding attracts more participants than more traditional sports such as baseball (Glader, 2007). Additionally, skateboarding and other "extreme" sports have come to represent creativity, cool, and youthfulness. Marketers knowingly use skateboarding to sell a wide variety of products such as soda, antiperspirant, and fast food to a youthful market (Browne, 2004; Howell, 2003). Skateboarding has influenced other popular cultural practices, including music, art, film, and television programming. In short, skateboarding is culturally powerful. How did it come to garner this cultural power? Who has supported and who has opposed skateboarding, and why? What are the cultural meanings of skateboarding? Who benefits from those meanings and who might be marginalized by them? These will be the questions that frame the following discussion. History, similar to most human events, can be interpreted from different vantage points. Thus, there is no singular history; instead, there are a variety of experiences that give rise to different histories of skateboarding. The examples used here are not meant to be conclusive. Instead, they represent the mainstream as well as North American trends and debates.

Skateboarding began in southern California in the 1950s, and its initial popularity occurred in the early 1960s when skateboards were first mass-produced. Since then, skateboarding has become a global phenomenon and has gone through peaks of popularity in each decade, but since the mid-1990s interest has been sustained. The activity has been shaped by key stakeholders, including the participants, promoters, parents, media,

Skateboarder Danny Way, 31, from Encinitas, California, jumps the Great Wall of China at Ju Yong Guan, north of Beijing, July 9, 2005. Way was attempting to break his own skateboarding records for distance (79 feet/24.07 meters) and unaided height out of a ramp. (AP Photo/Greg Baker)

medical associations, local governments, and youth cultural industry. Throughout the discussion of the development of skateboarding, one can note how these stakeholders and societal factors have impacted the meanings and styles of skateboarding.

1960 to 1966: sidewalk surfin'

Although people had created personalized wheeled-boards or makeshift skateboards before the 1960s, it was at this point that the mass market for skateboards began in earnest. Members of the California surfing community played a pivotal role in promoting the initial skateboarding industry. This market was fueled by several societal factors associated with postwar North America. First was an economic boom that provided more money and leisure time for people to participate in activities. Second was the growth and spread of suburbs and suburban leisure opportunities. Third, the "teenager" as a social category became prevalent, and industries actively catered to this age group. Simultaneously, there was a growing discussion about how young adults, especially males, were using their new leisure time and the lack of adult supervision or surveillance to ensure socially proper behavior. This was expressed in popular cultural media such as the film *Rebel without a Cause* (1955).

Skateboarding was initially promoted by surfers. Skateboarding was envisioned as an extension of surfing, riding a board on cement instead of water. By promoting skateboarding as a dry land alternative, the surfing industry was able to package a like-minded activity and enlarge its market. Because skateboarding's roots are based in both the California surfing scene and in the suburban youth pastime, there has been a tension between the individualistic and antiauthoritarian image of a surfer and mainstream market appeal of American suburban youth. This tension is embodied by the fact that from the very beginning of mass production, popular cultural industries have been integrally involved in the development of the image and technology of skateboarding (Chivers Yochim, 2010). Even though skateboarding is currently touted as an alternative to highly organized sport, where participants can control the activity, it nonetheless has a history of being supported and promoted by various industries that were interested in tapping into the youth market.

Three surfers—Larry Stevenson, Hobie Alter, and Larry Gordon—made a huge impact on skateboarding by creating a product, developing a skate team, taking that team on tours, and sponsoring competitions to promote their product In the early 1960s, Larry Stevenson started promoting skateboarding in his suffering publication, *Surf Guide*. In this way, he built surfers' interest. And it worked. In 1963, he created Makaha Skateboards and was the first to sponsor a team. Some of his sponsored skateboarders included Bruce Logan, John Fries, George Trafton, Wood Woodward, Torger Johnson, Jim Fitzpatrick, and Danny Bearer. These teams, like today, are used to market products, especially those associated with surf culture, as the demonstration team did after the screening of the movie *Surf Crazy* (Chivers Yochim, 2010). In addition, he sponsored the first skateboard contest held in Hermosa, California. His brand was extraordinarily successful, selling $4 million worth of boards in two years (Brooke, 1999).

Another surf industry leader, Hobie Alter, worked with Val's surf shop and Chicago Roller Skate company to sell boards and their components as a complete set. In 1964, he created a working partnership with Vita-Pakt Juice Company to create Hobie Skateboards. To promote the product, a team of surfers and skateboarders was put together, including Davey and Steve Hilton. This team went across the United States doing exhibitions linked with the screening of the legendary classic surf film *The Endless Summer* (Brooke, 1999).

Larry Gordon was part of Gordon & Smith, a surfboard company. Gordon conceptualized using fiberglass to provide more flexibility for skateboards. In the early 1960s, Larry partnered with Jim Hovde and created a company that produced Fibreflexes. They too put together a team of skateboarders for promotional purposes, including Willie Phillips, Mike Hynson, and Vince Turner (Brooke, 1999).

The surfing industry was also behind the first skateboard magazine, the *Quarterly Skateboarder*, an important venue for promoting the sport. Surfer Publications produced the first issue in 1965, right before the first wave of popularity ended, which reduced demand and resulted in only four issues being published.

The 1960s represented a shift in social perception from skateboarding as a childhood activity, much like roller skates and scooters, to a unique sport. Most of the early skateboards were flat and made of wood; the wheels were clay. At this point, skating was practiced on the ground; there were few aerial moves. Most tricks were called freestyle and had a wide variety of gymnastic qualities such as handstands or spinning moves. Skaters were often pictured barefoot, except when they were participating in slalom, which was also popular. There were few publicly sanctioned places to skateboard; therefore, it primarily occurred informally on paved streets, parking lots, playgrounds, and sidewalks. Some were skating in pools, but the focus was primarily on carving the terrain rather than getting airborne.

Most of the skateboarders covered in the early media and advertising were young, white males. However, there were girls' divisions in contests, and female skaters were given some media coverage. When ABC covered the American Skateboard Championships in 1965, they covered the girls' division, which featured the competition among Donna Cash, Wendy

Bearer, Colleen Boyd, and Laurie Turner. In addition, on its cover, *Life* magazine used a picture of Pat McGee, the national girls' champion, doing a handstand while riding her board. Yet from most accounts, the majority of participants during this period tended to be young, white, suburban men.

As participation rates continued to grow, skateboarding was increasingly integrated into popular culture. In 1964, Jan and Dean's song "Sidewalk Surfin" became a hit. The short film *Skaterdater* (1965) won best short at Cannes Film Festival in 1966. Skateboarding also gained national coverage when ABC's *Wide World of Sports* covered the 1965 American National Skateboard Championships held in Anaheim, California.

As skateboarding gained popularity among youth, there was growing public concern about the physical risks involved. Several national publications, including *Consumer Reports*, *Good Housekeeping*, and the *Los Angeles Times* covered stories on the hazards of skateboarding. Medical associations denounced skateboarding because of related injuries. Joining these concerns was public commentary on skateboarders' disorderly behavior, especially how they upset pedestrians and disrupted shopping experiences (Chivers Yochim, 2010; Weyland, 2002). In addition, proprietors were concerned about legal responsibilities and damage skateboarders might cause to their property. Not surprisingly, city governments started to debate banning skateboards, and many did.

By 1966, the first boom in skateboarding was over. The business and medical fields' disapproval impacted the support of local community councils and businesses, and likely led to its decline at the end of the decade. It didn't reappear until mid-1970s. This time period was clearly fraught with a multitude of political issues in the United States ranging from the Vietnam War, civil rights, and aftermath of Watergate. It may be that these issues dominated public discussions, pushing to the margins debates over young people's leisure activities, or it may be that many young people were intellectually and actively engaged in challenging the powers that be through direct political action, and thus had less time and energy for seemingly frivolous activities such as skateboarding.

1970s: rise in popularity: innovation and diversification

The mid- and late 1970s represent the expansion and diversification of skateboarding in both technology and style. With important innovations in board shape and size, the wheels, the bearings, the trucks, and safety equipment, the skateboarding industry grew as several new companies emerged. Pool skating also became popular during this period, which prompted the development of skate parks. In turn, there was diversification in the types and styles of skateboarding, from slalom and freestyle to more vertical styles used in pools, pipes, and ramps. *Skateboarder* magazine was resurrected, and mainstream media covered skateboarding again. All this drove skateboarding back into popularity.

Although there is not one single factor that accounts for the renewed popularity during the 1970s, most skaters acknowledge that technological innovation was significant. One key individual was Frank Nasworthy who, for personal use, envisioned using urethane instead of clay for wheels. Urethane allows for a smoother and more stable ride than clay, and it also provides skateboarders the opportunity to ride more varied terrain. But it wasn't for another two years, in 1972, that he and his friend Bill Harward decided to mass-market urethane wheels for skateboards. They were called Cadillac Wheels. Because they were more expensive and the popularity of skateboarding was still low, they did not catch on right away. But after two years of the wheels being promoted in California, they gained the attention of young skateboarders such that a market was created. Importantly, the existing surfing network helped re-establish skateboarding. Nasworthy used surfing connections to promote his wheels at surf shops that also

Downhill competition, 1970s. (Photo courtesy of Bobby Smith.)

carried skateboards. Nasworthy then joined Bahne, a company that made both surfboards and skateboards, to secure more capital to develop and market their wheels. The next versions of the Cadillac Wheels were not a success and other companies, such as NHS's Road Riders, started to develop better bearings systems and thus outperform Cadillac Wheels. Although Nasworthy and Bahne both eventually left the skateboarding business, their initial innovations led others to refine the technology, leading to better products for skateboarders (Brooke, 1999). George Powell created rounded edges on wheels, which made skateboards more responsive to various terrains (Davis, 1999). Trucks, the axle-like component that attaches the wheels to the board, evolved from roller skate trucks to those specifically designed for skateboards. Trucks allow for smooth riding and precision turning. With better wheels and trucks, higher speeds could be reached and controlled.

Other innovations occurred with new materials and board designs. Fiberglass, aluminum, plastic, and various layers of wood were used to create the board. The style of skateboarding impacted the shape. Freestyle boards remained about 24 inches long and 6 to 7 inches wide; downhill boards became longer, often 48 inches in length; and other boards became wider for more stability. In addition, there were many different variations

Freestyle competition, 1970s. (Photo courtesy of Bobby Smith.)

of these shapes, including the double-wide board with eight wheels (which never really caught on). Boards shifted from being flat to incorporating uplift at both ends, referred to as tails and noses, and became slightly concave. Surfing and skateboarding were still intimately connected during this period, with surfboard manufacturers creating some of the early lines of skateboards such as Bahne and Zephyr.

The 1970s was a time of experimentation and amalgamation of styles. Many of the styles developed during the 1960s, including freestyle, slalom, downhill, and pool skating, remained popular during the 1970s. While skateboarders continued to develop their skills in these various styles, the 1970s also saw the development of a more aggressive bank, ramp and pipe skateboarding which was the precursor to vertical style, as made popular by the Z-boys. The mid-1970s saw the style shift from the 1960s freestyle form to a more aggressive style that drew inspiration from some of the maneuvers being performed by the most progressive surfers of the day. Tony Alva, Jay Adams, and Stacy Peralta were at the forefront of this style, which was made famous by the movie *Dogtown and Z-Boys*.

Freestyle was composed mostly of dance and gymnastic-like moves while also drawing from traditions of longboard surfing. For example, the hang ten was riding with all 10 toes hanging over the nose of the board. Walking consisted of walking up and down the board while it was in

Pool skating, 1970s. (Photo courtesy of Bobby Smith.)

motion. Both of these tricks were common in longboard surfing. There were variations of wheelies in which the board was ridden only on one set of wheels such as the nose wheelie or the tail wheelie done with either one or both feet on the board. The daffy used two boards and combined a nose wheelie on one board with a tail wheelie on the other. A skater accomplished a spinner by jumping off the board, spinning his or her body 360 degrees, and landing back on the board. Skaters did lift their boards off the ground in the 1970s, but it was a different mechanism than current practice. The aerial was executed barefoot. The skater would place one foot on the nose and one at the tail, grab the edge of the board with his or her toes, and then jump and lift the board. The gymnastics-inspired moves included doing handstands on the board while it was moving; variations included a handstand wheelie or spinning the board 360 degrees. To do a V-sit or L-sit, the skater grabbed onto the board with his or her hands and then lifted and used his or her arms to hold his or her body's weight (Davidson, 1976). In freestyle contests, skaters were judged on their footwork, spins, handstands, multiple board tricks, and aerials. Freestyle differed from slalom and downhill skateboarding because it was done on flatland. These two styles were also popular.

Downhill skaters simply tried to gain as much speed as possible. Minimizing turns and adopting tucked body positions, some skaters reached speeds of 50 miles per hour. The most famous race occurred at Signal Hill in San Diego. The downhill races were created as a media event. ABC wanted a skateboard event for their show "The Guinness Book of World Records." The U.S. Skateboard Association worked with ABC and created Signal Hill Speed Run, which lasted from 1975 to 1978. In the first competition, Garrsion Hitchcock and Guy Grundy were the only two skaters who were fully prepared for the event. Hitchcock fell, and Grundy was clocked at just over 50 miles per hour. The event turned out to be dangerous but also spurred several adaptations of skateboard, including first street luge, and even the super ramped-up skateboards, which were actual enclosed vehicles with steering and brakes (Horelick, 2007). Slalom is similar to snow skiing slalom. Skateboarders created a course by simply placing a line of cans or cones on a downgrade with the object of weaving in and out of the cones as fast as possible.

While pools were skated in the 1960s, the practice became prevalent in the 1970s. During the water shortage of 1975 to 1976, many homes in southern California did not fill their pools, leaving them empty. Skaters would search out empty pools and then wait for the residents to go out of town, upon which the pool would be taken over for a skating session. Pool skating was frequently done illegally. Although probably not the norm for most skaters, these episodes were recorded and helped to create a public image of skateboarders as rebellious.

Pipelines that were used to transport water became another favorite of skaters during the 1970s. When they were empty, skaters rode the sides of the pipes, often taking their boards beyond the vertical point. Pipe skating was featured in magazines, especially the famous installation in Arizona. Other hot spots were the pipeline at Mt. Baldy in the San Gabriel Mountains of southern California and Camp Pendleton outside of San Diego.

The 1970s also witnessed a shift in style, one that featured more aggressive surfing moves, and it was embodied in a group of young males who were associated with a local surf shop called Zephyr. In 1968 two young men, Jeff Ho and Skip Engblom, entered a partnership and created Zephyr Productions Surf Shop in Santa Monica, California. During this time period, sections of Santa Monica were known to be crime-ridden and those sections referred to as Dogtown. Zephry's skateboarding and art styles took on the streetwise sensibility of Dogtown. From the Zephyr shop, skateboards were shaped, merchandise was sold, and a back room was used as an art studio

Arizona pipes, 1970s. (Photo courtesy of Bobby Smith.)

for their friend Craig Stecyk, who would later publish his work on the style and attitude of the Zephyr skaters, who were known as the Z-Boys. In addition, the shop served as a social conduit. During the day it was a place for the local youth to gather, and in the evening it was often used by young adults to socialize (Beato, 1999).

Zephyr was essentially a surf shop, but it became famous for being the center of the new aggressive skateboarding style, one that was drawn from short board surfing of Australian surfers. The Z-Boys would carve the blacktopped banks of playgrounds as if they were waves, positioning their bodies closer to the ground as they made sharp turns with their boards. Although primarily male, the ethnic demographics of the group was more representative of Los Angeles than the freestyle skateboarders. Tony Alva and Stacy Peralta are Latino, Marty Grimes is African American, and Peggy Oki and Shogo Kubo are Asian American. The Z-boys also included several members who are white such Jay Adams, Jim Muir, Wes Humpston, and Nathan Pratt. This group of skaters wanted to create a team and enter contests. Zephyr agreed to be the sponsor, and the Z-boys became the team name. The 1975 Del Mar (California) Skateboard Championships became the stage where they demonstrated the new style to a broader audience.

Part of the 1970s rebirth of skateboarding was the promotion of the sport, particularly via niche media such as skateboard magazines and movies. These products played an important role in developing the sport and its culture beyond local communities. In 1975, the magazine *Skateboarder Quarterly* was revived as *Skateboarder*. Steve Pezman, the publisher, also put out *Surfer* magazine. *Skateboarder* tended to focus on the California scene, and the magazine set the standard for the format that most others would follow. There were action shots, technical coverage of skills, coverage of interesting places to skate, profiles of skateboarders, and related commentary on the skateboarding social scene. In this way, the magazine was both descriptive of the activity and prescriptive in determining what part of the skateboarding culture was deemed important to cover. Importantly, this magazine published Craig Stecyk's depictions of the Z-boys, which helped to promote them and their style as cutting edge. Following the trend of the 1960s, niche films were created and shown in schools and community centers. Some of those included *Downhill Motion, Skateboard Madness*, and *Super Session* (Weyland, 2002).

Surf and skateboard companies had long created and used teams to promote their products, but now skateboarding was becoming an avenue to sell unrelated products to the youth market. The 1970s saw an explosion in interest by nonskateboard corporations as popular cultural industries attempted to take advantage of skateboarding's newfound appeal. For example, Pepsi Corporation sponsored a skateboard team, the Pepsi Pro Skateboard team. And sport promoter Bill Riordan, who had worked for tennis star Jimmy Connors, took up skateboarding because he believed, in his own words, "This thing is going worldwide. They sold 10 million skateboards in '75 ... Imagine, 300 million a year and nobody promoting it" (Deford, 1977). Riordan was developing a television show aimed at children that featured prominent skaters, including Ty Page, Pat Flanagan, Laura Thornhill, and Ellen O' Neal. One of the biggest music industry promoters of the 1970s, Don Branker, was also promoting skateboarding through contests and during his rock-'n'-roll music festival Cal Jam 2, which attracted 350,000 fans. He presented an exhibition by part of the California Free Former, including Laura Thornhill, Ty Page, and Bryan Beardsley. They performed freestyle and ramp skating (on a California Free Former's portable, see-through plexiglass ramp). This appeal also fueled the skate park construction business, which boomed in the mid- to late 1970s. Municipalities and private businesses started to create parks specifically made for skaters. These often included snake runs, bowls, and some ramps. By 1976, there were 200 of these parks across America. The first was built in Florida, and the next two were opened in California (Santa Cruz and Carlsbad). The trend was so popular that there were conventions organized around this business (Weyland, 2002).

The appeal of skateboarding was used to sell other youth-oriented products, for example, a line of bubblegum cards and stickers called All-Pro Skateboard that featured a variety of styles and skateboarders and had the official support of the International Skateboard Association. In addition, mainstream movies used skateboarding as a means to lure the youth audience. *Skateboard* starred U.S. teen idol Leif Garrett and featured skateboarders Ellen O'Neal and Tony Alva. The film relied on the skills of many other top skaters, including Jay Adams and Ellen Berryman. *Freewheelin* was another popular skateboard film (produced by an industry leader, Santa Cruz Skateboards) that starred skateboarder Stacy Peralta. The later part of the decade also saw the development of more theatrical skateboarding events and spectacles. In 1978, the production called *Skateboardmania* was created. The show used laser lights and a full loop ramp, and it featured glitter-costumed skateboarders such as Tony Jetton and Vickie Vickers, who were depicted in a battle between aliens and earthlings (Lucero, 2005). Skateboarding also was used in a made-for-television sport competition, the *Battle of the Network Stars*. Leroy Neiman, a famous artist of sports, created a painting called "Skateboard Boy." And many celebrities used skateboarding to promote their own popularity, including the 1970s celebrity icon Farrah Fawcett.

To help promote the sport and ensure its viability, many professional organizations were created. Most of these organizations were developed by business interests and sought to standardize contests, certify instructors, promote safety, and work with local governments to develop skateboarding. This included the Pro/Am Skateboard Races Association, the United States Skateboard Association (formed by Jim Mahoney), the California Skateboard Association, and the International Professional Skateboard Association. The promotion went beyond North America. For example, in 1975, Russ Howell and Stacy Peralta were part of a promotional team that toured Australia for six months (Brooke, 1999; Mortimer, 2008).

For a variety of reasons, the popularity of skateboarding started to wane in the late 1970s. This was reflected in the magazine *Skateboarder* shifting its focus to include other sports such as BMX. By 1980, it was renamed *Action Now*, but the newly envisioned magazine lasted only two years. One reason frequently given for the second decline in skateboarding popularity is the dissolution of the skateboard park industry. Insurance premiums were becoming too costly and forced many parks to close. In addition, youth industries began to shift away from skateboarding and toward roller-skating because roller-skating was believed to have a broader appeal (Chivers Yochim, 2010). With the withdrawal of significant funding from large corporations, skateboarding-specific brands were forced to redefine and remake the image of skateboarding and skateboarders.

1980s: taking it to the streets and keepin' it real

Skateboarding took a significant turn in style, culture, and global reach during the 1980s. After a lull in the early part of the decade, skateboarding was booming globally by the end of the decade. The reliance on surfing images and businesses was tempered as skateboarding took on an urban punk style, and former skateboarders began their own successful companies. The 1980s also witnessed a merging of surf and punk styles as the freestyle and ramp skating of the 1970s was modified to work in urban spaces, ultimately morphing into "street style" that has become the signature of skateboarding. The different styles that developed were shaped not only by the use of urban landscape or prefabricated ramps, but by the meanings these styles were given by the various stakeholders. As skateboarders began to take control of their industry and establish an identity different from the 1970s surfing inspired style, tensions arose around what constituted a "real" or "authentic" skateboarder.

debating authenticity

The withdrawal of mainstream corporate support from skateboarding in the early 1980s created a void, one that would be filled by those committed to skateboarding. Those who were willing to invest in skateboarding reimagined what skateboarding could be. The desire to refashion a skateboarding identity was shared by many, but what that identity would consist of was contentious.

This debate is clearly illustrated by the two main skateboarding magazines—*Thrasher* and *Transworld Skateboarding*—that developed during the 1980s. *Thrasher* was created by Fausto Vitello, who also owned Independent Trucks. *Transworld Skateboarding* was created by Larry Balma, who owned Tracker Trucks. It is important to note that they were using their media as a means to promote skateboarding and to promote it in a particular fashion, one that circulated their ideas and images of a real skateboarder. In other words, the authenticity debate has been, in part, manufactured by skateboard corporations as a component of their marketing campaign.

In 1981, Vitello created a skateboard magazine that emphasized a more punk, do-it-yourself (DIY) orientation to skateboarding. *Thrasher* claimed to be for "core" skaters and not big business, and its motto was "skate and destroy." Thus, Vitello packaged and sold a rebellious image that included embracing skaters such as Duane Peters, who embodied this image. In addition to covering the most proficient core skateboarders, *Thrasher* also featured new tricks, both local and global places to skate, as well as music and the social lives of skaters. To further encourage the growth of skateboarding, *Thrasher* supported many local competitions (Brooke, 1999; Mortimer, 2008).

Larry Balma and other skateboarding advocates such as Neil Blender and Grant Brittain were part of the organization United Skate Front, and in 1983 they started publishing *Transworld Skateboarding*. Their intention was to make skateboarding accessible to wider audiences, including more mainstream companies and parents who often oversaw what their children purchased. To differentiate their audience from *Thrasher*, they downplayed the antiestablishment ethos and took up the motto "Skate and Create."

competing styles

Not only was there a debate about what constituted a legitimate or authentic skateboarder, but there was a lively exchange and development of styles and techniques.

There was continuation of the range of styles created and developed in the 1970s such as freestyle, pool, pipe, longboarding, slalom, and ramp or vertical skating. The ramp and aerial style of skateboarding was most popular until the end of 1980s, when "street" style became prominent. Street style emerged from freestyle but was modified to blend with the urban landscape. Rodney Mullen's career exemplifies the transition from free to street style.

The ollie was the crucial technical invention that significantly changed both street and aerial or vertical (vert) style. Alan Gelfand has been credited with originating the move in the late 1970s, but it was not widely used until the 1980s. This move enables the skateboarder to propel the board off the ground. With this technique, skateboarders could now "jump" onto a variety of objects, and thus it provided the most important skill in the evolution of street skateboarding. Freestyle evolved aerially and was used on the street as well as in ramps and pools. On the streets, skaters were jumping onto objects such as handrails or parking blocks and then sliding their boards on them. Mark Gonzales and Natas Kaupas are key figures in creating street style of the 1980s. This period also saw the development of aerial vertical skateboarding, as exemplified by Christian Hosoi and Tony Hawk, which takes place on (and above) ramps, half pipes, and pools.

According to Stacy Peralta, when skateboarding slumped in the early 1980s, he began brainstorming with Vitello and Craig Stecyk about how to reinvigorate the market (Mortimer, 2008, Greenfeld, 2004). Their strategy was to make skateboarding more widely accessible while creating an antiestablishment form of cool. To do this, they promoted local types of contests, such as ramp jams staged in participants' backyards, giving the appearance of local as opposed to corporate control. They also worked at promoting street style skating to increase their consumer base; because it doesn't require special apparatus (in fact, one simply uses everyday elements of the street), more people could potentially participate. *Thrasher* started promoting street contests in 1983 via contests that purposely celebrated the more gritty and edgy elements of street skating by creating a harsh urban atmosphere by staging old cars and painted graffiti on ramps. Peralta claims that street style was not made by skaters, but by the industry in the early 1980s as a means to revitalize the market (Mortimer, 2008). As skateboarding in public spaces became more popular, numerous local ordinances were passed to make that practice illegal. Many business owners and pedestrians perceived public skateboarding as a nuisance and a liability. In response to this movement, one of the more popular bumper stickers declared that "Skateboarding is NOT a crime."

As some groups were trying to create an outlaw image, others were trying to create a mainstream one. Frank Hawk, father of skateboarding icon Tony Hawk, was a leading proponent of the latter. The senior Hawk was unimpressed by the level of organization of skateboarding competitions and wanted to create a more professional setting for his son and other young people who skateboarded during this period. In 1980, he created the California Amateur Skateboard league. In 1983, he created the National Skateboarding Association (NSA). Danielle and Don Bostick became deeply involved and ran the NSA with a goal of making it "more professional and more accepted ... similar to Little League" (in Beal, 1995). In response to such developments, Steve Rocco, a skateboarder and entrepreneur who later started World Industries and the notorious *Big Brother* magazine, created "hell tours" to challenge the bureaucratic and formal system of contests (Weyland, 2002).

As these groups were vying to establish the legitimate styles of skateboarding, one group was consistently excluded: females. Whereas the 1960s and 1970s skating establishment embraced female participants by providing opportunities to formally compete and by providing media attention, the 1980s emphasis on a street-wise and anti-authoritarian style marginalized females. In fact, most contests dropped the female category altogether, such that women like Cara-Beth Burnside had to compete in male divisions. Despite her high skill level, Burnside had to create her own company in order to support her career as a professional skateboarder. Skateboarding media very rarely covered females as competent skateboarders, emphasizing instead their role as a "skate betty": a groupie of the male skateboarders.

central role of the media

Media are not only crucial in promoting and circulating these competing images and narratives of an authentic skateboarder, they are central to the professional livelihood of skateboarders. Unlike many mainstream sports where athletes make the majority of their money based on performances in competition, skateboarders actually rely little on monies made from competition. Instead, they make the vast majority of their money through sponsorship deals with skateboarding-related companies; their salaries are highly dependent on their exposure in niche skateboarding magazines and videos. What is crucial in becoming sponsored is to be highly skilled and have a style that differentiates you from other skaters and, in turn, have a trademark style that becomes established and marketed through media exposure.

As many skaters recognize, there are literally thousands of highly skilled skaters, but only a few are provided with opportunities to gain widespread visibility. The industry, especially the media, are the ones who select the skaters and provide them with that visibility. This was especially true before more democratized forms of media such as the Internet were developed for the general public (early to mid-1990s). In addition, the industry has more resources than individual skaters, so it has more power to choose what types of skateboarding get support and media exposure. In the 1980s, several individual skaters (e.g., Christian Hosoi's Hosoi Skates and Steve Rocco's World Industries) recognized this, started their own companies, and began producing their own media in order to have more control over the sport. That trend boomed in the 1990s and has continued through today.

impact of videos

Thrasher and *Transworld Skateboarding* were the prominent magazines of the 1980s, but other forms of media were developed. Videos became one of the most powerful ways for companies or individuals to communicate. Initially, skateboarding videos were simply upgraded magazine advertisements that featured skaters performing tricks using a particular product. But they evolved to include story lines and soundtracks such that they became a means of transmitting skateboarding culture and the notions of authenticity. As technology became more affordable, individual skaters started using videos to document their local scenes. Videos remain a primary means of artistic expression and communication among skaters.

The company called Powell Peralta was at the forefront of revolutionizing the use of videos. The company was started in the 1970s by George

Powell; later in that decade, he signed on legendary skater Stacy Peralta. Peralta's original job was to be a team manager and work in promotions. He had several strategies, but the most noteworthy was his use of skateboarding videos. He developed the concept of telling a story, adding humor, and highlighting the personalities of the sponsored skaters as a central part of the videos. Peralta asked Craig Stecyk to join him in creating these videos (Dinces, 2011). Stecyk was the artist that photographed and wrote about the Z-boys (of which Peralta was a part) in the 1970s.

The Bones Brigade was the name of the Powell Peralta team. The name was derived from one of their members, Ray "Bones" Rodriguez. The team was a host of top talent of the 1980s, including Rodney Mullen, Tony Hawk, Steve Caballero, Lance Mountain, Ray Barbee, and Tommy Guerrero. These videos were immensely popular and have set the standard for the industry.

Their first video, *Bones Brigade Video Show*, surpassed their expectations and sold 30,000 copies. The popularity of this video led to producing several more. One of those videos, *Search for Animal Chin*, not only showcased the skaters' skills, but created a storyline that represented a rejection of authority replaced with a do-it-yourself (DIY) orientation and intrinsic motivation as the epitome of skating. Thus, authentic skaters needed only to rely on themselves and other skateboarders—not purchase equipment from companies that weren't run by and for skaters (Dinces, 2011). This insider narrative has been used by nearly every skateboarding manufacturer to present themselves as legitimate.

highs and lows

By the late 1980s, the popularity of skateboarding was at a zenith. Young people were taking it up more than ever, and top skateboarders were making hundreds of thousands of dollars per year. Skateboarding once again meshed with youth popular culture, especially music and fashion. Several punk and indie bands were known to be connected to skateboarding such as the Circle Jerks, Suicidal Tendencies, and Social Distortion. Duane Peters, a top skateboarder, transitioned into lead singer of several punk bands. Christian Hosoi was known to hang out with members of the bands Red Hot Chili Pepper and Beastie Boys (see sidebar on songs that feature skateboarding). Hosoi was so popular with young people that he had lucrative sponsorships from nonskateboard companies. And skateboard companies such as Vision had crossover success with their line of clothing marketed for nonskaters. Again, popular films picked up on the trend and featured skateboarding such as *Thrashin'* (1986) starring Josh Brolin with Christian Hosoi, Lance Mountain, and Tony Alva doing the skateboarding scenes and *Gleaming the Cube* (1989) starring Christian Slater with skateboarding appearances by Tony Hawk and Rodney Mullen. Two films that had skateboarding sequences were also popular. *Back to the Future* (1985) starred Michael J. Fox riding his futuristic skateboard, and *Police Academy 4* (1987) featured the Bones Brigade skateboarding team.

The largest U.S.-based skateboard corporations intentionally marketed globally, specifically to Japan, Australia, and Europe. The European Cup was established, and there were several international competitions such as the one in Munster, Germany, which was one of the most internationally vibrant skate competitions throughout the late 1980s and 1990s.

The global success helped secure financial benefits for the five dominant skateboard corporations: Independent, Powell Peralta, Santa Cruz, Tracker, and Vision. An internal struggle started to surface as a growing backlash against those corporations began to boil over as many skaters pointed to monopoly-like practices. One rallying cry of the late 1980s and early 1990s was to "keep it real" and not to "sell out" to the commercialization process. Frustrated, some of these skaters went on to create their own companies. One classic example is Steve Rocco. He was one of the skaters who aggressively challenged the status quo of the 1980s. In 1987, with very little capital, he started World Industries and soon after, many skaters followed his lead and started their own companies. Rocco and World Industries defied many of the 1980s traditions; particularly, he employed self-deprecating humor and developed cartoon graphics that are now rather common. He went against the grain of representing skateboarding with ferocious images such as skulls, crosses, and bones. His audaciousness continued throughout the 1990s with the establishment of the notorious skate magazine *Big Brother* (discussed in next section).

The 1980s is marked by the skateboarding industry intentionally creating an identity separate from surfing and further, claiming that this new distinctive identity represented an authentic skateboarder. Not surprisingly, different groups had different standards of what constituted a real skateboarder, sparking a debate within the industry and skateboarders themselves about what constituted a legitimate skateboarder. Skateboard companies that seemed to market for a mainstream audience by doing such things as selling their wares in national department store chains, as was the case with Vision, were often met with a backlash from skateboarders who saw them as selling out. As previously discussed, the niche media, including skateboard magazines and videos, played a crucial role in promoting particular forms of authenticity as they highlighted different lifestyles of a skateboarder. The contention was primarily in the degree of rebelliousness that should be embraced. The industry had to play a balancing act between appealing to a broad audience for financial reasons and simultaneously appealing to "hard core" skaters in order to "keep it real."

But another lull in popularity occurred primarily due to the worldwide economic recession. At the end of the decade, skateboarding was going through tough times with serious internal divisions, a sharp decline in the number of participants, and the infamous reputation of slacker punks for those who did participate. Few could predict that in 10 years, skateboarding would be a more powerful and positive cultural symbol than ever.

1990s: x marks the youth market spot

Not only did skateboarding rebound in the 1990s, it became one of the most powerful symbols of the hip, independent, and entrepreneurial teenager. This cultural appeal is exemplified by Tony Hawk being one of the most popular athletes, as well as by Nike trying to enter the skateboarding market. By the late 1990s, skateboarding was ubiquitous in commercials as it was used to sell everything from soda and fast food to antiperspirants and cars. An overview of the dynamic changes within skateboarding provides some backdrop to this meteoric rise.

Even though the early 1990s economic recession impacted the popularity of skateboarding, many professional skateboarders were picking up on the momentum set by Steve Rocco, who was a leading example that skateboarders could successfully develop and run their own businesses. In fact, Mark Gonzales was directly encouraged by Rocco to start his own company. Gonzales created Blind, which was a spoof on his former sponsor's company, Vision. Ed Templeton, a highly talented skater of the 1980s and 1990s, started the company Toy Machine. He eventually merged with another upstart company, Foundation, which was created by Tod Swank. Their joint venture was called Tum Yeto. Tony Hawk and fellow Bones Brigade skater Per Welinder started Birdhouse. Another Bones Brigade rider, Lance Mountain, started the company The Firm. Girl and Chocolate Skateboards were formed by a partnership of Rick Howard and film director

Skater jumping a fire pit in Venice Beach, California, 1990s. (AP Photo/Mark J. Terrill)

and producer Spike Jonze, who later had mainstream success with films such as *Being John Malkovich* and *Adaptation;* he was also the producer of MTV's skateboarding-informed humorous film series called *Jackass*.

With the infusion of numerous skateboarder-run industries, the marketplace became more competitive, and marketing strategies became more creative. Many of the newly formed companies branded themselves as authentic by highlighting their skateboarding roots (and challenging mainstream ethos by promoting an independent, creative and rebellious ethos) (Beal & Weidman, 2003).

Again, Steve Rocco was a leading force of this change. The magazine *Big Brother* was introduced in 1992 to compete with *Transworld Skateboarding* and *Thrasher*. Yet similar to those two magazines, which were owned by people who also ran skateboard companies, *Big Brother* could be used as a means to sell World Industries products. It was notorious for controversial "drugs, sex, and rock-'n'-roll" content. It was commonly sold with privacy wraps, and in 1997 Larry Flint Publishers took it over. Throughout the 1990s, several skateboarding magazines were started, including *Slap* and *Heckler*. Other magazines were created to promote the skateboarding aesthetic and lifestyle such as *Vapors* and *Strength*.

A skateboarder goes airborne off a bench at San Francisco's Pier 7, June 29, 1999. (AP Photo/Pico van Houtryve)

a skateboarding aesthetic

Most skateboarders gain recognition from their peers through demonstrations of skill and personal style, and this is often recognized through photographs in magazines or videos, not through competitions. The significance of one's personal aesthetic for peer acceptance and, ultimately, potential financial rewards is imperative. As noted previously, those in the industry have a huge influence on what types of skills (street style versus longboarding) and demeanors (e.g., risktaking and antiauthoritarianism) are sponsored and the manner in which those are eventually represented artistically. Importantly, grassroots skaters also create representations of

Jessica Krause competes in the All Girl Skate Jam. (Patty Segovia, allgirlskatejam.com)

skateboarding and distribute those on the local scene. The neighborhood skateboard shop became the hub where locals would share their 'zines and videos. 'Zines have been pervasive (Brooke, 1999; Weyland, 2002). They are inexpensive and locally produced magazines that focus on the area skate spots, people, music, and art. As video technology became more accessible, skateboarders often create their own videos and, similar to 'zines, these are shared and helped develop an aesthetic. Videos often include several short episodes pieced together of urban skateboarding, mainly in "illegal" settings that are exemplified by being chased by police or harassed by an annoyed adult. In addition, the inclusion of skateboarding through poverty-stricken areas is common. The effect is to present skateboarders as creatively navigating dangerous territory (Dinces, 2011). Although national industries have more influence over the dominant skateboarding aesthetic, there is an exchange of ideas across geographical regions. For example, nationally distributed magazines comment on local 'zines. A synergy is formed around an aesthetic that highlighted urban or street skateboarding, risktaking, rebelliousness, and masculinity (Beal & Weidman, 2003; Rinehart 2005). This aesthetic influences what is considered an authentic skateboarder and subsequently pushes those who do not fit this aesthetic to the margins, most notably females. In response to this, females, such as Patty Segovia, started to photograph and write about female skateboarders so that they would be included in the skateboarding media. Additionally, in 1997, she created a competitive forum to highlight female talent, called the All Girl Skate Jam (AGSJ). It originated in southern California but now sponsors competitions throughout North America.

The emphasis on artistic expression has generated support for related careers. Several skateboarders have become recognized artists, including Ed Templeton and Mark Gonzales (more on the institutionalization of skate art in chapter 3). Music has always been used to set the tone for skate sessions and has been incorporated in videos. In the 1980s, the connection to punk became pervasive, and skaters like Duane Peters made a career in music. The music and skateboarding connection became institutionalized through various festivals that were created in the 1990s, including the Warped Tour, All Girl Skate Jam, and the X Games.

mainstream corporations going after the youth market

Skateboarding has historically been associated with youthfulness. But in the late 1970s and into the 1980s, the skateboarding industry made a concerted effort to market a unique identity built around rebelliousness. In so doing, they packaged a whole lifestyle—including music, art, and fashion—around skateboarding. In the 1990s, this "packaged" lifestyle made the demographic easily targeted by those outside of skateboarding. In particular, skateboarders represented a demographic that was appealing to other businesses because it was large in number and in wealth (Browne, 2004; Chivers Yochim, 2010). The story of the X Games exemplifies this trend.

espn

The X Games are the creation of the media group ESPN, which is owned by Disney Corporation. ESPN is primarily a North American phenomenon but does have global reach. In the early 1990s, ESPN wanted to target a younger audience with its new station, ESPN2. The managing director, Ron Semiao, had observed a variety of magazines focusing on specific alternative sports. He imagined programming that would appeal to this younger demographic by capturing the individualistic and antiauthoritarian nature of these sports along with their subcultural music and language (Browne, 2004). As Semiao mused, "There was a lifestyle and culture attached to these guys and no one had tapped into . . . I thought, 'Let's create the Olympics of these sports' " (Wise, 2002 para 19). In 1995, the Extreme Games were launched (later renamed the X Games), and vertical skateboarding became a signature event. A crucial issue for ESPN is how to mass market an event that is supposed to be antiauthoritarian, a hurdle that Nike also faced.

nike

Nike also wanted to reach this desirable demographic, so they tried to enter the skateboard shoe and soft goods market in 1997. They released clever television advertisements that showed mainstream athletes such as tennis players, golfers, and joggers being chased out of public spaces by police and harassed by the general public. The byline was "What if we treated all athletes like we treated skateboarders." Although the advertisements were well received, the first generation of Nike skateboard shoes was not a big hit. Many skateboarders were skeptical of a mainstream "outsider" company entering the market (Beal & Wilson, 2004). Nike had to adjust its marketing strategy to gain the trust of skateboarders. It used insider distribution strategies and sold shoes only through skateboard shops. It eventually developed a talented team that included Paul Rodriguez, Jr., also known as PRod. Additionally, Nike gained credibility by sponsoring "insider" skateboarding-related art exhibits such as *Beautiful Losers* (Atencio & Beal, 2011). By the mid-2000s, Nike was no longer seen as the untrustworthy outsider, but as an avid supporter.

The ability of skateboarding and other extreme sports to reach the highly coveted young male audience instigated a proliferation of soft goods that would represent this lifestyle. For example, there were three main brands of skate shoes in the 1980s, and by the end of the 1990s, there were over 50. More importantly, mainstream companies were packaging a variety of products under the extreme sport moniker to attract that audience. Different corporations diversified their products to include media, music, and fashion, but used extreme sports as the thread that connected them. Marketers refer to this as a seamless presentation of products in venues of teen life. For example, David Pokress, the director of global brand management for Activision (producer of Tony Hawk's computer games), stated, "The idea wasn't just to represent skateboarding as a game—we wanted to capture the whole lifestyle. I listen to a certain kind of music, I wear a certain kind of clothes, I hang with a certain crowd of people" (p3pr28, Edgers, 2002). The president of SONY Pictures Digital Entertainment concurred: "We view their customers as our core demographic for many of our properties—our games, films and music are integral part of their lives as they express themselves through action sports" ("Quiksilver launches," 2002). In the early 2000s, there were 1,141 registered trademarked products with *extreme* in their name (Browne, 2004). As cultural industries were using skateboarding to sell their products, the skateboarding industry was (and continues) working to develop a cohesive front to have some control over the future and image of the sport.

skateboarding organizations

Skateboarding organizations exist to promote the sport. They do this primarily by increasing the number of participants and the respect of the sport. If participation grows, then the market grows and moneyed interests are easier to secure. Organizations have worked to ensure access for skateboarders by changing laws to make skateboarding legal, building skate parks, and securing financial support through sponsorships.

In 1995, the International Association of Skateboard Companies (IASC) was formed. This alliance allows corporations to work toward a mutual goal of promoting the sport. They collaborate to create strategies that benefit skateboarding. One of the most crucial things they have done is to change the legal status of skateboarding in the state of California. Before the bill (AB 1296) was passed, skateboarding was not only illegal in public spaces, but the local government or businesses were liable for injuries that occurred on their property. The bill made skateboarding was a hazardous activity, meaning that individuals assumed the risk when they participated, much like bicycling. With the liability risk lifted, a new wave of skateboard parks were built, both public and private. The legal shift in effect decriminalized the activity, allowing infrastructure investment. Public skate parks in California increased from fewer than 200 to over 2,000 from 1995 to 2005 (Howell, 2008). Other private groups, such as Vans, were building skate parks in shopping malls. Top corporations are influential members of ISAC, and they have been successful in developing the sport globally. One of their promotional tactics was to establish an annual international skateboarding day (June 21). They helped to establish the Skateboard Hall of Fame, which is housed in the facility called Skate Lab in Simi Valley, California.

In the early 1990s, the National Skateboard Association (NSA) underwent a transformation. Danielle and Don Bostick, leaders of the NSA, knew they had to change to address both professional skateboarders and corporate interests. Additionally, they needed to develop globally. In 1994, World Cup Skateboarding (WCS) was started. Like most governing bodies, it tries to standardize the sport by creating formal rules and means of ranking professionals. When the WCS sanctions a contest series, the points a skateboarder accumulates from that contest count toward his or her overall ranking. In 1996, the International Gravity Sports Association (IGSA) was formed. IGSA organizes events specifically for downhill skateboarding as well as street luge and, similar to other governing bodies, it has established a professional event circuit and athlete ranking system.

Skateboarding organizations and events are designed with athletes at the fore. Indeed, skateboarders are central to the whole industry. In the 1990s, street style became the dominant form. Some of the top street skaters included Eric Koston, Kareem Campbell, Chad Muska, Geoff Rowley, Daewon Song, and Elissa Steamer. Vertical and ramp skating became the showcase media event. Tony Hawk, Bob Burnquist, Danny Way, Andy MacDonald, Cara-Beth Burnside, Jodi MacDonald, and Jen O'Brien were consistently top performers.

2000s: institutionalization, diversification, and globalization

One of the key markers of the first decade of the twenty-first century is the large number of people participating in skateboarding, making it one of the top 10 most popular sports in the United States. Between 1998 and 2007, the number of skateboarders in the United States skyrocketed by 74 percent, up to over 10 million (Badenhausen, 2009) with some estimates as high as 12 million participants (Clemmitt, 2009). Today, skateboarding embraces more than the youthful and rebellious. For example, organizations for older skaters are being formed, like Skate Moms and Geezerskates. Masters divisions, often called legends, are included in competitions. Longboarding, downhill skateboarding, and pool riding are all experiencing a resurgence of popularity. Additionally, skateboarding has become institutionalized in the form of international governing bodies, industry, and media. This diversity in styles as well as the institutionalization of skateboarding has become a global phenomenon. While there has been room made (in the form of thriving markets) for a variety of interests, the historical struggle over who gets to control the standards and future of skateboarding remains. Central to this struggle is ensuring an "alternative" reputation while simultaneously becoming more mainstream. Even though these political tensions are apparent, for all intents and purposes, it appears that skateboarding has moved beyond its boom and bust cycles and is becoming an institutionalized part of the sport landscape.

institutionalization

Skateboarding's stakeholders realized that they needed to cooperate in order to move beyond the boom and bust cycles of previous years, and sustain growth and popularity. As noted previously, one of the key moves was the development of the International Association of Skateboard Companies (IASC) in 1995. One of its primary goals is to provide infrastructure to encourage participation, which in turn provides a consumer base for the industry. Thus, the development of legal places to skate has been one of the organization's main objectives. With the success of the IASC in dismantling legal barriers to public skate parks, the Skate Park Association of the United States was founded. These organizations provide plans and strategies for those who want to build public skate parks. In 2009, there were over 2,100 skate parks in the United States, a substantial increase from

Amateur winners of the All Girl Skate Jam, 2002: Monica Shaw, Lyn-Z Adams Hawkins, Iris, Becky Syracopolus. (Patty Segovia, allgirlskatejam.com)

the 165 parks 12 years earlier (Clemmitt, 2009). The significance of providing legal and safe places to skate is further exemplified by two prominent foundations, the Rob Dyrdek Foundation and the Tony Hawk Foundation, which provide further support and funding to communities.

The institutionalization and popularization of skateboarding can also be observed in the recent trend toward incorporating skateboarding into the curriculum of physical education classes. Skate Pass is a company that has created curriculum to incorporate skateboarding into classes. Skate Pass was developed by professional snowboarder Eric Klassen with his former physical education teacher Richard Cendali (Loew, 2008). The Rob Dyrdek Foundation provides free skateboards for this program. Skate Pass is being used in 31 U.S. states as well as in Canada, Germany, Singapore, and the Dominican Republic. Deck manufacturer Paul Schmitt has designed an educational curriculum, CreateaSkate, that has students apply science to build a skateboard.

In 2006, Jeffery Stern, the parent of a skateboarder, wanted to create a competitive interscholastic skateboard league for high school youth, and he wanted to make it a team sport. It started in Los Angeles in 2007. High school administrators wouldn't financially support the league because of liability issues, so it was formed as a not-for-profit that took on the liability and was called the California High School Skateboard Club. Like many other club sports, the students coached themselves. Stern worked with the Tony Hawk Foundation to help set up the league. In addition, Nike sponsored the high school club's event, and provided shoes for the top prize (Higgins, 2007, June 6). The following year, Stern transformed this league into the National High School Skateboard Association, which is independent from the high schools and continues to be sponsored by Nike as well as Powell, Red Bull, and the X Games. (Nealon, 2009).

While people are integrating skateboarding into school systems, others are trying to institutionalize skateboarding at another level: the Olympics. The Olympics have incorporated other "action sports" such as snowboarding, mountain biking, and most recently BMX. Its intention is to develop a younger audience. Thus, it is not surprising that with the increased popularity of skateboarding the Olympics have shown an interest. To be included in the Olympics, a sport has to be governed by an international body that the International Olympic Committee (IOC) recognizes, which skateboarding did not have in the beginning of the twenty-first century. The IOC suggested that other governing bodies of wheeled sports such as cycling or rollersports become the international representative of skateboarding (Higgins, 2007, June 14). This reignited the debate in the skateboarding community about who was going to control skateboarding and to what degree it should be involved in mainstream sport competitions. Although there has not been overwhelming grassroots support for Olympics involvement, the industry did not want to lose control to another governing body. In other words, if there was enough momentum to push skateboarding into the Olympics, then the industry wanted to steer the direction. The International Skateboarding Federation (ISF) was created in 2004. For this organization to be recognized by the IOC, it had to have international partners (as of 2010, there were currently 70 countries from 5 continents) and hold world championships. The ISF even became a member of the IOC-sanctioned World Anti-Doping Agency (WADA). Throughout the late 1980s until more recently, the competition that the skateboarding community saw as its world championships was the World Cup in Munster, Germany. Although previous competitions have been labeled world championships, none were organized by an IOC-recognized governing body. In 2009, the ISF held the world championships in Boston by sanctioning the already established Dew Tour (which is owned in part by the media group NBC). Twenty-eight countries and 140 athletes were represented. Whether skateboarding ever becomes an

Olympic sport, there are now many national and international skateboarding organizations such as the European Skateboard Association, United Kingdom Skateboarding Association, Canadian Amateur Skateboarding Association, National Skateboarding Association of South Africa, Skateboarding Turkey, and Indonesia Skateboarder Association.

role of media

Mass media has been a fundamental driver in the institutionalization of skateboarding. Niche media (e.g., magazines, videos) has always had the role of shaping the image of skateboarding and selling that image to the skateboarding audience. Since the advent of the X Games (see chapter three for more details of the X-Games), however, mainstream media has played a significant role in establishing widespread appeal.

In addition, the media not only broadcast competitions to international audiences, but also worked to promote a particular lifestyle. At the forefront of this is the role of MTV. The network recognizes the value of skateboarding for attracting young viewers. They have collaborated with various skateboarders to promote comedy and reality programming. Bam Margera, the prankster of the skateboarding world, released a series of skateboarding videos called CKY (Camp Kill Yourself). MTV noticed his slapstick humor, and the organization drew on the style and humor of CKY videos to create the comedic series called *Jackass*. The show was a hit and led to three feature-length *Jackass* films. MTV played off the success of that program and worked with professional skateboarder Rob Dyrdek to create the series *Rob and Big*, which focused on the friendship of Rob and his bodyguard, "Big." After that series ended, MTV featured another Dyrdek program called *Fantasy Factory*, which displayed the comical workings of his corporation and how it developed different products, including the world's largest skateboard. MTV also worked with Ryan Sheckler in creating the reality show *The Life of Ryan. Skater Girls*, a reality program that follows the lives of female skateboarders, is their latest venture. In 2008, MTV's investment in action sports was also established in a new company, Alli Sports, which was created through a partnership with NBC Sports. Alli Sports showcase different action sports events, multimedia platforms to show events, a web presence as a source of news coverage, and an e-commerce site.

In the 2000s, several films focused on the culture of skateboarding. Most significantly was the award-winning documentary *Dogtown and*

Z-Boys, which told the story of the rise of aggressive street skateboarding. This 2001 film was directed by Stacy Peralta and partially funded by Vans. Another award-winning film to feature skateboarding was Gus Van Sant's 2007 adaptation of the novel *Paranoid Park*, which addresses the life of teenagers in Portland, Oregon. Another film highlighting urban teenagers' relationship with skateboarding is Larry Clark's 2005 film *Wasssup Rockers*. Mainstream authors also used skateboarding as the means to convey teenage culture in the 2000s. Nick Hornby, the author of *About a Boy* and *Fever Pitch*, wrote the 2007 novel *Slam* in which a teenage boy partly relies on the image of Tony Hawk as counsel for his own transition into adulthood.

The one media form that has been credited with engaging mainstream audience with skateboarding is video games. In particular, Tony Hawk's series of video games has been a perennial top seller since it came on the market in 1999 (Iwata, 2008). His games have generated over $1 billion (Kelly, 2010). These games represent well-known skate locations and have avatars of other famous skateboarders.

As skateboarding has entered mainstream imagination, the ability of traditional sporting manufacturers to find credibility has increased. As noted before, Nike had difficulty entering the market in the 1990s as it was seen as a predatory outsider. Today, it is seen as legitimate. In the early 2000s, Adidas also entered the market, gaining legitimacy by sponsoring skateboarding icon Mark Gonzales. Reebok entered the market by sponsoring Stevie Williams. The global worth of skateboarding is an estimated US$5 billion per annum (Glader, 2007; Howell, 2008). Skateboarding is definitely being sold as part of a lifestyle where the soft goods speak to more than skaters (Iwata, 2008) and the biggest revenue streams are shoes (Browne, 2004). Styles such as "skurban," a fusion of urban and skateboarding, speak to the lifestyle combination of fashion, music, and art that is being sold. This integration of a whole lifestyle is illustrated by Vans's latest flagship store, the House of Vans, which opened in 2010 in Brooklyn, New York. This space incorporates indoor and outdoor skate parks, original artwork, and music venue, as well as houses its East Coast marketing offices.

diversification

As noted above, businesses have been able to capitalize on the popularity of skateboarding. Organizations and media that promote females have also proliferated. These organizations hold contests, provide skateboarding lessons and camps, and provide educational literature. As noted earlier, Patty Segovia created the All Girl Skate Jam in the 1990s, and it continues today with female contests having been incorporated into the Vans Warped tour in 2006. Girl Riders Organization (GRO) started in 2006. Skateboard Moms started in 2004 and features the Mighty Mama Skate-a-Rama event (see chapter three or more details). Female-oriented media has also proliferated. The Skirtboarders are a Canadian female skateboard crew that has its own website. Chica Rider is a Mexico-based website, Skatergirl is a UK-based website, and The Girls' Skate Network is a U.S.-based website. All are dedicated to promoting female skateboarding. Organizations such as Adaptive Action Sports, which promotes skateboarders with disabilities, are being formed, and skateboarders with disabilities are being included in competitions. Including older age groups is also gaining popularity, as can be seen by Skateboard Moms and Geezerskates. Additionally, different styles of skateboarding are being promoted such as mini-ramp, longboarding, pool riding, and downhill skateboarding. This proliferation of styles and increased access for various groups of people is good for business and for those who want to skate.

global reach

The skateboarding industry has a history of trying to establish a global market, but it was during the 2000s that this goal was firmly established. Media corporations like Disney (who owns ESPN and the X Games) along with sporting goods corporations like Nike, Adidas, and Vans all used their long-standing international structures to promote their products. The X Games started global competitions in the late 1990s with the X Games Asia. They've also created competitions among countries in their X Games Global Championships. Woodward Camps—which provide training for skateboarding, BMX biking, and other winter action sports—were started in Pennsylvania in the 1980s and have expanded globally. A camp was opened in Beijing, China, with the help of the Chinese government, which subsidized the 2005 project with the equivalent of US$12 million, and the government invested millions of dollars in a three-acre skateboard park in Shanghai, where the X Games Asia takes place (Higgins, 2010, May 26). In 2008, the Maloof Money Cup was established, offering the largest cash prize (160,000 US$ per event) in the history of skateboarding. The Maloof brothers own a National Basketball Association (NBA) franchise along with a Las Vegas casino; they have expanded into skateboarding, and now they are taking the event to South Africa.

power struggles continue

As global corporations began to gain more power in the industry, skateboarders pushed back, continuing a trend that was set back in the 1980s when skaters started to run their own companies. In the 2000s, skaters are organizing and demanding better working conditions and pay in mediated skate competitions. In the 2002 X Games, the skateboarders—led by Andy MacDonald, who founded the United Professional Skateboarders Association (Jim Fitzpatrick was the executive director)—organized and threatened a strike if they did not receive better compensation. ESPN met their demand (Siler, 2003; Wise, 2002). Women skateboarders were also pressing for their needs to be met. The X Games did not include women's skateboarding events until 2003. These women did not receive television coverage and were paid minimally, especially compared to the men. In 2005, an advocacy group for females, the Action Sports Alliance, was formed by professional skateboarders such as Cara-Beth Burnside, Mimi Knoop, and Jen O'Brien. They partnered with other organizations such as the Women's Sport Foundation to help advocate for equitable pay and television coverage for female skaters. They too threatened to boycott if ESPN did not provide more equitable support (Higgins, 2006, July 26). In 2007, female skateboarders' pay was increased. In 2009, they were finally awarded prize money equal to their male peers.

Another attempt at challenging the X Games lock on skateboarding was Rob Dyrdek's creation of the Street League, which debuted in 2010. It features street-style skateboarding and has one of the largest financial payouts. More significantly, it provides revenue sharing for the athletes who compete. While it rewarded the street skateboarders well, it also required them to sign a contract that does not allow them to compete in the three biggest competitions, the Maloof Money Cup, the Dew Tour, and the X Games. In this way, Dyrdek was trying to create the most prestigious tour. Top skaters such as Chris Cole and Nyjah Huston have signed on with Dyrdek.

top skaters of the 2000s

With the number of skateboarders continuing to grow, so too has the number of highly talented participants. Some of the most consistent male performers in street include Chris Cole, Nyjah Huston, Ryan Sheckler, and Sean Malto. With respect to vertical skaters, Pierre Luc Gagnon, Danny

Songs in the Key of Gravity

These represent a range of songs dedicated to skateboarding

Song	Year	Artist
"Sidewalk Surfin' "	1964	Jan and Dean
"Skateboard"	1978	Jefferson Starship
"Skate and Destroy"	1985	The Faction
"Life on a Skateboard"	1993	Altered State
"Skateboard"	1995	Beatnik Termites
"Go Skate"	1997	Suicidal Tendencies
"My Skateboard"	1997	The Aquabats
"Mondo Aggro"	2000	Code 13
"Downtown in Dogtown"	2001	Fu Manchu
"Heaven Is a Half Pipe"	2001	OPM
"Sk8er Boi"	2002	Avril Lavigne
"Skateboard Anarchy"	2002	JFA
"Born to Skate"	2003	The Stupids
"Separation of Church and Skate"	2003	NOFX
"Kick, Push"	2006	Lupe Fiasco
"Skate Town"	2006	Van Stone

Way, and Sandro Dias have been outstanding. High-level female street skaters include Marisa Dal Santo, Leticia Bufoni, Alexis Sablone, and Vanessa Torres. In vert, top performers include Cara-Beth Burnside, Lyn-Z Adams Hawkins, and Gaby Ponce.

3. venues for creativity: sites, events, and competitions

this chapter focuses on particular sites, events, and competitions devoted to skateboarding. It is important to note, however, that the creative ethos of skateboarding is about continually finding new places or constructing one's own skate spot. Skateboarders often seek out architecture that wasn't originally designed for skateboarding but lends itself to good runs or obstacles that require new tricks. Skateboarding magazines often feature road trips of skaters as they cross Canada or the United States looking for ideal spots and challenging structures. While most skaters have favorite spots in their local communities that remain largely unknown except among small groups of their skateboarding friends, certain spots have gained cultural status (mainly through skateboarding magazines, videos, and video games). Their iconic status is more about what the spot symbolizes than whether it is well designed. The sites need to embody the ideals of skateboarding: creativity, freedom, and a do-it-yourself (DIY) ethos (Beal, 1995; Borden, 2001; Chivers Yochim, 2010). Therefore, parks managed by city or corporate authorities, which have rules and regulations, generally have less status than spots such as stairways or plazas, which skaters have identified, or parks that the skaters have created and manage themselves. Not only are spots imbued with this ethos, but the culture of skateboarding promotes a variety of creative endeavors in the use of these found and constructed spaces (Borden, 2001). For example, art and music are commonly incorporated into celebrating the spot, event, or competition.

burnside bridge (portland, oregon, united states)

One renowned skate spot is underneath the Burnside Bridge in Portland, Oregon. In 1990, a few local skaters decided they needed to create a space to skate and were looking for a location that would stay relatively dry, as Portland is a rainy region. Ultimately, they settled on the space underneath the Burnside Bride. It was a rough area, consisting mainly of vacant lots used for drug and prostitution transactions. The project started with a few skaters using cement to create a bank against the wall, and then other skaters heard of the new place and started to add more elements. Highway construction was going on close by, and the skaters convinced a cement company to dump its leftover cement from the day's work so that the skaters could use it to build further features. With the supply of fresh concrete, the park grew quickly, and elements such as bowls were constructed. The success triggered others to contribute time and equipment such as a backhoe (and an operator) to help build bowls. Although the park continues to evolve as skaters add new or change old features, Halloween has been deemed the park's birthday, and big celebrations happen each year (Willis, n.d.). The park is free and has no formal regulations. Interestingly, though, the park is established enough within skateboarding culture and the Portland community that is has become legally classified as a tax-exempt charitable organization ("Burnside Skatepark," n.d.). Over the years, the Burnside skate park has garnered much publicity and acclaim; it features in Tony Hawk's video games and appeared in *Paranoid Park*, a movie about a teenage skateboarder produced by Gus Van Sant in 2007. With the widespread popularity of the Burnside skate park, it is not surprising that skateboarders from across the United States and around the world visit the park when in they are in the Portland area. Yet local skateboarders have been known to carefully regulate participation by visitors.

skatopia (rutland, ohio, united states)

Skatopia was originally developed by Brewce Martin in 1995, and since then, the skaters who visit assist in the maintenance of the facilities. It covers 88 acres of forest in Rutland, Ohio, and contains bowls, pipes, pools, and ramps. Martin's goal was to create a place of freedom, a utopia, and in his utopian vision there are no rules. When skaters visit, they are welcome to camp on the site. Martin and his son live on the property and run a skateboarding museum (Binelli, 2008). Every summer since 1996, they have held a Bowl Bash, which is a music festival and skateboarding party. Skatopia has become a culturally renowned spot through media buzz. It has been featured in skateboarding magazines as well as in popular literature such as *Rolling Stone*. It features in the Tony Hawk Skateboarding Underground 2 video game, and the movie *Skatopia: 88 Acres of Anarchy* documented the development and culture of this unique site. On its official video website one skater, Ryan, declares Skatopia ". . . a skateboarding Mecca. It is a million dollar skatepark right here in Brewce's backyard" (http://www .skatopiathemovie.com/).

brooklyn banks (new york, new york, united states)

Often, skate spots were not initially built with skateboarding in mind; rather, they are public spaces that inspire the imagination and challenge the skills of skateboarders. One such site is the Brooklyn Banks in New York City, a plaza located under the Brooklyn Bridge on the Manhattan side. The space is not used by many pedestrians, and skateboarders utilize the smooth and gradually curved embankments lining one side of the plaza, long handrails, benches, and planters (Chiu, 2009). Its status is legendary; as noted by *New York Times* writer John Branch, "The Brooklyn Banks is to New York skateboarding what Harlem's Rucker Park is to basketball" (2010, para 13). In 2004, the city wanted to enhance the plaza by adding features to diversify the populations that could use it. A local group of skateboarders, led by Steve Rodriguez, worked with the city to modify those plans so that its use for skateboarding would not be diminished (Branch, 2010). Since 2005, it has been the site for the Back to the Banks competition. Recently, renovations on the bridge began, and the plaza was slated to be the staging site for construction, which would prevent skateboarding. Another compromise was reached to keep half of it open until the repairs are finished, which is scheduled for 2014.

love park (philadelphia, pennsylvania, united states)

In the cases of the Brooklyn Banks and Burnside Bridge, city authorities ultimately worked with skateboarders to find a mutual position on the use of public space, a position that included skateboarders. This was not the case for Love Park in Philadelphia. This park is located across from the city hall in Philadelphia, and until the mid-1980s was used by a wide variety of people. But in the late 1980s and throughout the 1990s, this park became a popular skate spot and ultimately a skateboarding cultural icon as it was featured prominently in skate magazines, videos, and Tony Hawk's video games. The popularity of Love Park was a major factor in drawing the X Games to Philadelphia in 2002 and 2003. Nonetheless, city officials banned skateboarding and spent large amounts of money to beautify and alter the landscape to make it inaccessible to skaters (Howell, 2005). This decision was hotly contested. Importantly, this disagreement was not simply skaters on one side and business elite on the other. The business community was actually split. Those with interest or investments in the entertainment industry, such as ESPN, found skateboarding in the city positive for economic development. The more traditional business elite, on the other hand, argued that skaters in the city center were disruptive to commercial flow. As in many other cases, the compromise was to build a separate skate park outside of the city center.

skate parks by celebrities and companies

Another spin on skate spots is to create a park made specifically for skateboarding and draw on famous public skate spaces for the design. This is what Rob Dyrdek, a well-known skateboarder and TV personality, did when planning a skate plaza. It's called a plaza because it pulls together elements of street skating and not ramps, pools, or bowls. Dyrdek borrowed design ideas from some of the most popular street spots such as Pier 7 in San Francisco and Love Park (Heizer, 2004). He became part of the planning of this park, which is located in his hometown of Kettering, Ohio, when youth and city parks and recreation officials identified a need for a community skate park. Dyrdek worked with these groups to design and build a 40,000-square-foot park, which opened in June 2005. The city paid two thirds of the cost, and Dyrdek's foundation picked up the other third. The park is free to the public. This concept of a skate plaza inspired Dyrdek to design and develop five more in his current place of residence, Los Angeles. These are much smaller and designed with the aim of creating safe and legal places for people to skate.

In 1998, the shoe company Vans opened a 30,000-square-foot skate park in a shopping mall in Orange, California. This park was a significant investment for Vans and thus signaled that the market for skateboarding was on solid ground. Unlike the other parks mentioned in this chapter, this one is intended to make money for the owners in order to cover the rent of the facility. However, the park also features other consumer opportunities, such as the purchase of Vans merchandise and an arcade. The skate park provides a broad range of elements ranging from street, pool, and ramp features. They, too, borrowed a pool design from an iconic 1970s and 1980s park, the Upland Pipeline.

The Berrics is a skate spot with a competition that is bolstered by a web page and has evolved into a brand. The Berrics is run by professional skaters Steve Berra and Eric Koston. *Berrics* is a combination of their names, Berra and Eric. The Berrics's competitions and website has become one of the most popular, which has facilitated other ventures highlighting DIY projects by and for skateboarders. Most recently, in the summer of 2011, Berra and Koston, along with a coalition of private and public entities, opened a public skate plaza in Los Angeles.

The Berrics started as a private skate park. Berra and Kosten bought a warehouse in Los Angeles in 2004 and created an indoor park that became the underground hot spot where top skaters would be out of sight from sponsors. This carnival-like place that Berra and Koston created for their friends to skate inspired Rob Dyrdek to create a television show about his business operations called Fantasy Factory (Nieratko, 2009). Berra has a long history working in film as well as being a skateboarder, so dramatic staging was part of the package (Dougherty, 2009). As Berra and Koston integrated media, the Berrics evolved into a public realm. With a website giving virtual access to the facility, anyone could watch the antics of professional and amateurs who entered the Berrics. Berra recalls his motivation to make the space more public:

> I had just come off a year long journey of directing a film. It was an extremely tough experience; the toughest experience I've ever had professionally. When it was over, I started coming to the park again and was just completely in awe of everyone's skating. I remember sitting there thinking that if I get this much enjoyment out of this, what would a skater from Nebraska (where I'm from) get out of it. I was aware that I'm on the other side of the looking glass and that I have an opportunity to bring this to all those skaters who were like me, the ones who dreamed of California and hanging out with the pros and seeing what they were like. I wanted to make that happen. I wanted to fill that void. ("The Berrics," 2009)

Additionally, the competition called Battle at the Berrics is a single elimination tournament of a game called S-K-A-T-E, which is similar to the game H-O-R-S-E played with a basketball. It's a one-on-one contest where each skater is trying to outdo his or her competitor trick for trick. One skater starts by doing a trick, and the second skater needs to do the exact trick and land it. If the second skater is unsuccessful, that skater gets an *S*. The first skater to spell out S-K-A-T-E loses. If the second skater successfully lands the trick, the first skater gets to initiate the trick to emulate until he or she makes a mistake. Then the lead is given to the second skater. The Battle of the Berrics features 32 of the best skaters, is broadcast on the park's website, and is one of the most watched skateboard contests.

international skate spots

There are many other notable spots to skate both in the United States and internationally. Locations such as the south bank of the Thames River in London and the Marseille Skate Park in France have been an integral part of the international and their respective national skateboarding scenes for decades. One of the most notable spots to skate in Montreal is called the Big O. This 50-foot-long and eight-foot-high concrete tube structure was built as a pedestrian tunnel for the 1976 Olympics in Montreal. In 2011, the city's professional soccer team was expanding their stadium, and the Big O was in the way. Local skaters organized and made a request to the soccer club, the Montreal Impact, to save their legendary spot. The management agreed that the Big O had cultural value and moved the 17-ton concrete pipe, intact, just 25 yards to preserve it (Hamm, 2011).

Other skate spots have been built more recently for the explicit purpose of skateboarding and to draw major events to the region. For example, Black Pearl Cayman Island is one of the largest skate parks at 62,000 square feet of skateable surface, including bowls and pipes. This facility also includes lessons and camps for all levels of skateboarders. With this investment, the Cayman park is setting itself up to be a destination spot for tourism and competitions. Another large park with a multitude of features for street, pool, and ramp skating is located in Calgary, Alberta, Canada. Shaw Millennium Park is nearly 75,000 square feet. Shanghai also has invested heavily in a massive skate park called SMP that includes ramps, a variety of bowls, and a street plaza. Additionally, it has a separate competition area with spectator seating. This park serves as the location for the Asian X Games and the Shanghai Showdown. Amazing Square in Tokyo is another enormous park that provides a variety of elements and is open 24 hours a day. Barcelona's central distract plazas, including the museum of contemporary art (MACBA), have become meccas for street skateboarders.

skateboarding events: music, art, and camps

As skateboarding has grown and evolved, it has solidified an image around creativity, freedom, and a do-it-yourself (DIY) ethic. The industry's goal has been to create a unique sport and an associated youthful lifestyle to help capture a market. As one skateboard media executive explains, "The mainstream thing hadn't worked, so we just terrorized. That was how we saw we could promote the sport" (Greenfeld, 2004, 69). Obviously, the plan worked; the market for skateboarding and its lifestyle has been sustained and developed globally. Skateboarding competitions and other events have played an important role in the development of a skateboarding lifestyle that incorporates art and music as complementary forms of DIY and creativity.

Music festivals have included skateboarding, for example, Cal Jam music festivals in the 1970s and Tony Hawk's BoomBoom HuckJam in the 2000s. One of the most prominent music festivals to feature skateboarding is the Warped Tour. It was started by Kevin Lyman, who had worked previously with skateboard and music shows and decided to package the idea. In 1995, Lyman signed Vans as the major sponsor. Featuring an array of bands popular among skateboarders (e.g., Pennywise, Blink 182) as well as skateboarding and other action-sport events, the Warped Tour has grown every year since its inception (Browne, 2004). Skateboarders are often passionate about particular styles of music such that many skateboard magazines have a regular column that profiles music. Skateboarding is also being incorporated into theater and dance productions. For example, *Traces*, a theatrical production by Montreal-based 7 Fingers Production, uses skateboarding to help convey its theme of urban acrobats.

skateboarders as artists

One of the main tenets of skateboarding is that it is an art form. Besides the act of skating, many skaters have expressed their artistic side by producing artwork for their decks or promotions. A handful of skateboarders have even gone on to develop a career in the fine arts. Ed Templeton has become a well-respected painter and photographer. His work depicts everyday lives of ordinary people. His work has been exhibited throughout the United States and Europe, and was featured in a book, *Cemetery of Reason* (2010), which documents the art show held in Ghent, Belgium's museum SMAK (Stedelijk Museum voor Actuele Kunst). Another one of his shows,

"My Soul Is Worried Not Me," was exhibited at the Nils Staerk Gallery in Copenhagen. Templeton has also written an autobiographical book told through his art and family letters, *Deformer* (2008). He is the coeditor of an arts magazine, *ANP* (the Artists Network Project), and he started his own artzine called *Mothball*. He also started and owns the skateboard company Toy Machine.

Tommy Guerrero grew up in San Francisco, California, and was a member of the famous Powell Peralta Bones Brigade. He started the skateboard company Real in 1990 with Jim Thiebaud. This initial venture has evolved into Deluxe Distribution, which also owns the brands Spitfire, Anti-hero, and Krooked (Deberdt, 2011). In an interview with a San Francisco public radio station, Guerrero said that he started skateboarding at nine years of age and that he has been playing music since he was 12 (Curiel, 2011). Guerrero plays the guitar and is a composer. Early in his career, during the mid-1980s, he was a member of the band Free Beer, and later he played with Jet Black Crayon. In 2002, he connected with three other top skaters—Ray Barbee, Matt Rodriguez, and Chuck Treece—to form the Blktop Project. They toured and put out an extended play record (EP). His most critically acclaimed music has come as a more mature solo artist. His style fuses many types of music, from soul to funk and jazz. When asked what his inspiration is, he replied: "Maybe late sixties, early seventies Brazilian music—when bossa nova fused with funk and soul. Guys like Jorge Ben" (Deberdt, 2011, para 8). His music is only instrumental. He has had his songs featured on the TV shows *Queer as Folk*, *Sex in the City*, and *CSI: Miami* (Curiel, 2011, para 3). *Rolling Stone* magazine named his 2003 album, *Soul Food Taqueria*, as second on its best of 2003 album list. His latest album is *Lifeboats and Follies*.

The Soul Artists of Zoo York were a group of graffiti artists and skateboarders who lived in the New York City area in the 1970s. Initially, the group primarily consisted of graffiti artists. The Soul Artists were started in the early 1970s by Marc Edmunds, whose tag name was Ali. Edmunds came up with the term *Zoo York* to describe the unusual and interesting culture of the city. Other well-known artists in their crew included Zephyr and Futura 2000. Andy Kessler was the most well-known skater of the group; others included Ricky Mujica and Jaime Affoumado. During the 1970s, Manhattan was not known as a good skate destination, but the crew managed to find spots or create temporary ramps from wood they "borrowed." The mixing of the graffiti artists and skateboarders was facilitated by the fact that many of the skaters tagged, and many of the artists rode skateboards. So they often met in Central Park and socialized. The skate crew grew to 15 people by the late 1970s. Edmunds published a zine, *Zoo York*, in which he fictionalized competitions between skate crews. In doing so, he established a reputation for the Zoo York skaters as tough and rebellious. Throughout the 1980s, the crew broke up, either going different directions or dropping out due to drug abuse. Nonetheless, those who survived became artists, and Kessler designed skate parks (Browne, 2005). In 1993, Rodney Smith, who had run a company out of New York called Shut Skates, reorganized and created Zoo York Skateboard Company with Eli Gasner and Adam Schatz (Brooke, 1999). The original crew had mixed emotions about Smith, who was not associated with them, appropriating the name without reference to its origin (Browne, 2005). Kessler died in 2006.

Skateboarding as a form of art is taken seriously and is actively supported by the industry. In the past two decades, there have been numerous local and regional art exhibitions featuring skateboarders' work or the use of skateboards as art. *Beautiful Losers* is one particular exhibition that has gained mainstream recognition. It opened in 2004 and was billed as a multimedia art exhibit that features art from "street culture." The exhibit included installations, sculpture, drawings, graffiti, paintings, toys, graphics from magazines and album covers, film, photography, skateboards, and an actual skateboarding apparatus, a ramp-like bowl, which was used as part of the exhibit. The work of skaters Ed Templeton and Mark Gonzales was also displayed. The industry is aware of the cultural appeal skateboarding and art have. One apparel company, RVCA, supports an artist network program with a quarterly publication called *ANP*. Additionally, Nike was one sponsor of *Beautiful Losers* and more recently supported the creation of a skateable art installation at the Museum of Contemporary Art–Los Angeles called *Art in the Street*. Oakley has sponsored the annual *Love and Guts* skate/art show since 2005.

Until recently, skateboarding has commonly been represented as a white sport. To counter this perception, art exhibits have been used to provide the history and perspectives of ethnic minorities in the sport. In 2010, *Ramp It Up: Skateboard Culture in Native America*, was exhibited in Washington, DC at the Smithsonian National Museum of the American Indian. Also in 2010, an exhibit featuring the history of African Americans in the sport, *How We Roll*, was shown at the California African American Museum.

One example of a skate and art festival is Tha Hood Games, which was created by Keith Williams, an art educator from Oakland, California; Karl

Watson, a former professional skateboarder; and Barbara Murden, a social worker. The impetus was the lack of diversity that Watson experienced at the X Games, and the trio's vision was to create a positive skateboard experience for inner-city neighborhoods. The first festival occurred in Oakland in 2005 and has since extended throughout the San Francisco Bay area, Los Angeles, and Las Vegas. Along with skateboarding, youth exhibit their artwork, music, and fashion designs. In 2011, the African American Art and Culture Complex in San Francisco hosted a multimedia exhibit entitled *Tha Hood Games: Kids, Community and Comrades* to accompany the skate event (Gonzalez, 2011, July 7). Camp Woodward has donated a scholarship for a participant. To come full circle, the X Games now include a series of events during the competition called the Hood Games Xperience.

Camp Woodward is a prime example of how the industry has grown by creating engaging opportunities for its participants. Skateboarders who attend the camp learn skateboarding skills from experts, and they are introduced to skateboarding's broader culture of music, art, and media. Camp Woodward was originally established as a gymnastics camp in Pennsylvania in the 1970s. Despite thriving for most of the decade, the camp started losing customers as the 1980s neared. In an effort to attract new customers, the camp owners decided to add BMX biking to their repertoire in 1982, skateboarding in 1987, and inline skating in 1992 (Browne, 2004). They have since added cheer, snowboarding, and digital media camps. Today, Camp Woodward is renowned for providing excellent training facilities for skateboarding and other action sports. In addition, they have an educational program for high school students based at their California location (with a semester abroad at their Beijing site). Camp Woodward facilities are now found at five campuses: the original in Woodward, Pennsylvania; Woodward West in Tehachapi, California; Lake Owen in Cable, Wisconsin; Woodward at Copper Mountain in Colorado; and Woodward at Beijing in China. With the support of DC Shoes, Woodward West also houses one of the few permanent MegaRamps; the Woodward West facility also serves as a site for professional competitions. Camp Woodward has several partners in promoting their brand. Fuel TV, an action sports channel, has a TV series about the happenings at the original Camp Woodward. These camps have tapped into (and simultaneously helped to develop) a thriving youth market by providing high-quality facilities and staff, and by creating an atmosphere that integrates sport and digital media, meeting the interests of that audience.

A newly painted and resurfaced outdoor vert ramp is seen at Camp Woodward, June 22, 2005, in Woodward, Pennsylvania. This outdoor vert is ready for the Gravity Games, a made-for-TV competition featuring skateboarders and bikers scooting up and down ramps to soar high into the air. (AP Photo/Carolyn Kaster)

skateboarding contests

There are literally hundreds of skateboarding contests throughout North America and many more globally. The ones included here are some of the longest-running events or those with a high profile for professional skaters. Importantly, major media groups as well as the skate industry have invested heavily in promoting skateboarding by engaging audiences with top talent and festival-like atmospheres.

The vast majority of people skateboard as a recreational pursuit; they simply enjoy the activity and don't expect to, or aspire to, get paid. For those who try to make it a career, the line between amateur and professional is not clear. Amateurs get some compensation, usually free equipment, clothing, and some paid travel expenses. But skateboarding does not provide them with enough money to live on. Generally, being a professional skateboarder means that you are being paid to compete, although most of the funds come through securing sponsorships as opposed to earning money in competitions. Companies that produce skateboarding equipment and apparel sponsor a wide variety of people, but the companies decide who represents them as "professional" or as "amateur." Because of this, professional status is tied to what image or persona the company is trying to create. They obviously choose talented people, but they also choose team members based on their personalities and skateboarding styles.

tampa am and tampa pro

Tampa Am and Tampa Pro are series that originated from the Skate Park of Tampa (SPoT), which was started by local skateboarder Brian Schafer in the early 1990s. Both the contests and the facility are renowned. Tampa Am has been hosted at SPoT since 1993 and is one of the largest amateur contests. In 2001, Schafer and business partner Rob Meronek took their show on the road by creating an international amateur series called the Damn Am. In addition to several locations in the United States, other event sites are in Canada, China, and the Netherlands. The Damn Am now serves as the gateway for skaters to reach the Tampa Am. The partners' professional competition series, Tampa Pro, has been going annually since 1994.

When Brain Schaefer was 21 years of age, he convinced a warehouse owner to rent the facility to him. That was in 1993 and now, nearly 20 years later, Schafer is still using that warehouse to run the business and the park as well as the professional and amateur competitions held there (Putnam, 2006). According to skateboarder and ESPN commentator Chris Nieratko, "For skateboarders, The Skatepark of Tampa is our Disney World; the greatest place on earth" (2011, para 1). The park has been featured in two Tony Hawk video games. Like other cutting-edge venues, it now includes a building that houses music and art shows in the Transitions Art Gallery, and it has a bar and café called Bricks along with its own skateboard shop.

the all girls skate jam

The All Girls Skate Jam (AGSJ) is a professional and amateur series for females. It was initiated by Patty Segovia, who was skateboarding during the 1980s when the industry paid little attention to female skaters. Frustrated by the lack of media coverage and professional support available to female skaters, Segovia created the all-female event. The first AGSJ was held in 1990 in Reno, Nevada, and it became an annual event in 1997 as the female skateboarding market started to gain momentum. Like many other tours, the AGSJ provides more than a competitive arena; the AGSJ runs camps and works with other community groups to provide skateboarding lessons for girls. AGSJ contests are held throughout the United States and

Spain. In 2004, AGSJ competitions were incorporated into the Warped Tour, providing females with more global exposure.

the x games

The X Games are the most prominent series of skateboarding competitions to date because of the event's longevity and commercial viability. The X Games has the largest audience of any skateboard competition, thus providing a significant stage for the athletes to demonstrate their skills and in 2010, over 35 million people in the United States and over 382 million worldwide watched some part of the competition (Gonzalez, 2011, June 6). The X Games were started by the network ESPN (which is owned by Disney Corporation) in 1995 with the explicit goal of reaching a younger demographic (Browne, 2004; Pickert, 2009). Originally a U.S. event, the X Games have recently expanded their global outreach with the Asian X Games, which are held annually in Shanghai, and a winter version held in Tignes, France. Organizers are planning on adding three more international events and calling the series Global X (Higgins, 2011). Like other contests, X Games also include a cultural festival and will highlight the host city's unique culture in the new Global X.

Jake Brown is cheered as he competes in the Skateboard Big Air competition, August 8, 2004, at the X Games in Los Angeles. (AP Photo/Ric Francis)

Skateboarding has been an integral event in the summer X Games since the beginning. Since 1995, the X Games have had several different types of skateboarding competitions, including vert, street, park, best trick, big air, and the skate game (a version of the popular basketball game H-O-R-S-E). To provide the most spectacular performances, the big air event is held on the MegaRamp. However, the big air event has been controversial because only a few athletes regularly train for it (due to lack of access to facilities), and injuries during the competition are often life threatening. For example, in 2007, Jake Brown fell 45 feet, was knocked unconscious, and recovered from a bleeding liver, bruised lung, cracked vertebrae, and broken wrist (Higgins, 2009). Television programs around the world covered this jaw-dropping incident. Despite some questions regarding the safety of the event, the spectacular nature of the big air competition and industry support has kept the event in the X Games schedule. In an effort to keep up with the latest trends in skateboarding culture, the X Games schedule continues to evolve. In 2003, women's vert and street events were added, but vert was later dropped in 2011. Performing for a global audience, many skateboarders seek to perform new feats and break records at the X Games. Indeed, it was during the 1999 X Games in San Francisco that Tony Hawk landed his renowned 900, catapulting him to iconic status.

the gravity games, dew tour, and gatorade free flow tour

Trying to compete with the ESPN X Games format, NBC created the Gravity Games, which existed from 1999 to 2006. NBC differentiated its offerings from the X Games by sponsoring a series of events as opposed to an annual event. In 2005, the Dew Tour was started, and later it affiliated with MTV and created the platform Alli Sports to operate the Dew Tour as well as several other action sports competition series. The tour has five stops throughout the United States and attracts some of the top talent. It also sponsors a popular and expansive amateur tour, the Gatorade Free Flow tour.

street skating events

One of the more recent street competition series is the Maloof Money Cup (MMC), which was established in 2008. The event offers the biggest cash prize, paying out $160,000 to the winner in 2011 and putting up $1 million for any competitor who wins four titles. Before establishing the MMC, the Maloof brothers were already in the sport and entertainment business, owning the National Basketball Association (NBA) franchise the Sacramento Kings as well as a resort and casino in Las Vegas. The first MMC event was held in Orange, California, and the second was in New York. The competition series continues to expand and now includes Washington, DC, and Kimberly, South Africa. Recently, MMC started a tour with several stops throughout the United States and Canada. The MCC tries to distinguish itself by asking skaters to help make decisions about the organization of the events, including who is invited. Geoff Rowley, a highly talented and famous skateboarder, was hired to design the street courses. As many other skate corporations do, the Maloofs promote skateboarding by building parks for local communities and distributing skate gear to young children.

In 2010, Rob Dyrdek—with support from IMG, the largest sport agency in the world—created the Street League. The most recent iteration of a competition series, the Street League features street-style skateboarding on different skate plazas that are built by the Dyrdek Foundation. It has one of the largest financial payouts. But more significantly, it provides the athletes who compete with opportunities for revenue sharing from merchandise sold. While it rewards the street skateboarders well, it also requires them to sign a contract that does not allow them to compete in two of the biggest competitions, the Maloof Money Cup and the Dew Tour. It allows for participation in the X Games because Street League is televised on ESPN (which owns the X Games). Recently, Dyrdek and Maloof have been increasing competition for talent by providing more financial rewards (Higgins, 2010, October 15). Currently, both the Dew Tour and X Games have larger audiences at the events and on television, and that exposure draws skaters to those games. The impact of exclusive contracts on the success of each contest series remains to be seen.

pool events

While most of the bigger competitions focus on street and vert competitions, a renewed interest in pool skating has found a home in the Pro-Tec Pool Party, which has been held annually since 2005 at the Vans Skatepark in Orange, California. It features the combibowl (two bowls connected in the center) that was designed to emulate the famous Upland Pipeline skate park. This event draws top talent; even those who don't specialize in pool skating—for example, Tony Hawk—join the competition.

Soul Bowl, Huntington Beach, California. (AP Photo/Sean DuFrene)

longboarding events

Another form of skateboarding that is making a strong comeback is long-boarding. One specific derivation of this is downhill longboarding in which skaters can reach speeds of 60 miles per hour. Competitions at Signal Hill (in southern California) during the late 1970s were the first to feature both styles of downhill skateboarding, one in which the athlete is standing on the board and the other where the athlete is lying down, often referred to as street luge (Horelick, 2007). Grassroots skateboarders have been doing downhill ever since, and stories of skaters "bombing hills" remain legend in the northern California cities of Berkeley and Santa Cruz as well as the southern California cities of Malibu and Laguna Beach. In the 1990s, enthusiasts put together an amateur organization, The Northern California Downhill Skateboarding Association, to develop a community, but professional downhill skateboarding has only recently begun to pick up speed in North America. The International Gravity Sports Association runs a world cup series, and their events have been more popular in Europe. One of the most popular North American events is the Maryhill Festival of Speed. This competition takes place in rural Washington on a 2.2-mile road that features 25 curves. Over 200 longboarders from around the world participate in this annual event (Higgins, 2010, July 20).

A competitor races downhill on a longboard during the Britannia Beach Classic held in Britannia Beach, British Columbia, just north of Vancouver, May 29, 2011. The longboard classic brings racers from around the world to compete in a race that sees them hit speeds of up to 60 miles per hour on a skateboard. (THE CANADIAN PRESS/Jonathan Hayward/AP Photo)

The beauty of skateboarding can be showcased in competitions. Importantly, skateboarders do not rely on competitions to prove their worth. Instead, reputations are made primarily through video or photographic documentation that is distributed in magazines and via Internet. Also, most skateboarders do not make money from competitions. Instead, skateboarders make most of their money through sponsorships; the more media exposure an athlete gets, the more the sponsor pays that athlete. Few athletes such as Tony Hawk, Danny Way, and Bob Burnquist make a good living from these events. Moreover, most skaters don't participate in formal competitions; instead, they spend their time finding their own skate sports as well as creating their own venues and styles.

4. pioneers and heroes

skateboarding has attracted many passionate and creative individuals, as well as colorful characters and personalities, who have contributed to the growth and development of the sport. The 19 people included in this chapter are not necessarily the most talented (although they are certainly highly talented) or the most beloved skaters; rather, they have had a large impact on the culture of skateboarding. They have shaped styles, trends, and attitudes. Their influence is heightened because of the connections they have in the industry and media, giving their story widespread recognition and thus effect. Concomitantly, southern Californians get featured most since this has been the hub of skate industry.

patti mcgee (1945–)

McGee was a pioneer for women in skateboarding. She was the U.S. national skateboard champion in 1965. She was the first female to be professionally sponsored (by Hobie skateboards), and she toured the country doing skateboard demonstrations. She was featured on the cover of the May 14, 1965, *Life* magazine. In addition, she was the first female to appear on the cover of a skateboard magazine, *Skateboarder*. In 2010, she was inducted into the Skateboard Hall of Fame.

McGee was born on August 23, 1945, in Santa Monica, California. According to McGee, she was "in the right place at the right time" (McGee, 2009, 323) for developing skateboarding skills. Her mother encouraged and supported her participation in sports and physical activity. During her youth, she was an avid water sport athlete who competed in swimming, sailing, and surfing. In 1962, she started skateboarding. She and her brother Jack supported each other's athletic pursuits. Her multifaceted interests and skills included her love for speed; in 1965, she set the record for speed on a skateboard as she was being pulled by a motorcycle

(McGee, 2009). Her commitment, family support, and access to the southern California surf and skate scene all merged to enable her to become the most recognized female skater in the mid-1960s.

Her skateboarding fame led to other opportunities, including appearances on TV shows such as *The Tonight Show* and the *Michael Douglas Show*, where she demonstrated her skateboard skills. She also appeared in television commercials and worked as a stunt double for several beach films that targeted teenagers (McGee, 2009). Her work in and related to skateboarding stopped when the first wave of popularity came to a close in the late 1960s.

She left southern California to live in northern California, specifically the Lake Tahoe region, where she picked up snow skiing. She worked in the arts trade and ultimately moved to Arizona, where she ran a trading post. She works with her daughter, Hailey Villa, in a clothing business called First Betty (playing off the term *Skate Betty*, which refers to a female who is part of the skateboarding scene). McGee continues to skateboard on a regular basis and remains involved in the skateboarding culture and industry (Lannes, 2010, Nov 7).

jim fitzpatrick (1948–)

Fitzpatrick played a pivotal role in promoting skateboarding. In the early 1960s, he was a skilled skateboarder sponsored by Makaha skateboards. But his more significant impact has been in coordinating and organizing the professional field of skateboarding, especially the International Association of Skateboard Companies (IASC), which was founded in 1994.

Fitzpatrick was born in southern California on February 10, 1948. Living in the San Diego area as a child, he and his friends created makeshift skateboards. His father was a documentary filmmaker and moved his family closer to Hollywood. They arrived in Malibu at Topanga Beach when he was 12 (Mortimer, 2008; Lannes, 2011). It was here that he connected with Larry Stevenson, a pioneer in both surfing and skateboarding. Stevenson published *Surf Guide* and created Makaha skateboards. Stevenson invited Fitzpatrick to join the Makaha team. In 1964, the 16-year-old Fitzpatrick was part of the Makaha team that spent six weeks travelling to contests and exploring new terrain in various European cities (Mortimer, 2008; Lannes, 2011).

With few opportunities for pursuing a career in skateboarding during the late 1960s, Fitzpatrick left the Makaha team after the European tour and focused his energies on developing his adult life. After graduating from high school, he worked in the film industry. But in 1968, his father suddenly died; the following year, he got married. He and his wife decided to go to Italy to be educated in Montessori school philosophy and curriculum. They returned to the United States and opened their own school in Santa Barbara, California, in 1975. It wasn't until the late 1980s that Fitzpatrick reconnected with skateboarding (Lannes, 2011).

In 1987, he was hired by Powell Peralta (also based in Santa Barbara) to work as a writer and support its media productions. In this role, he helped promote the Bones Brigade and worked with Craig Stecyk and Stacy Peralta. Fitzpatrick left Powell in 1993, but he continued his work developing and promoting the industry as a whole. In 1994, he founded the International Association of Skateboard Companies. One of IASC's key accomplishments was the campaign to change liability reclassification of skateboarding in the state of California so that it was a "hazardous recreational activity" similar to bicycling. With this reclassification, skateboarders assumed individual responsibility while riding a skateboard and thus were unable to sue if they were injured while participating. This created new opportunities for both public and private groups to invest in skate parks, and a new boom in construction occurred. Fitzpatrick has been involved in other organizations, including the United Professional Skateboarder Association that was intended to advocate on behalf of professional skateboarders. In addition, he was centrally involved in creating USA Skateboarding, a governing body that was formed by the skateboarding industry in an attempt to keep control of the sport during a time when other governing bodies were vying to be the officially recognized governing body by the International Olympic Committee (IOC).

His promotion of skateboarding extends into the educational realm, as he has written several books on skateboarding, including biographies of Tony Hawk and Shaun White. His educational bent should not be surprising since he has committed most of his adult life to Montessori pedagogy and the education of children.

russ howell (1949–)

Russ Howell dominated freestyle skateboarding in the mid-1970s, winning numerous competitions as well as setting the record for the number of continuous 360s performed and the longest handstand on a skateboard. He started skateboarding in 1958 and he also surfed, snow skied, and practiced gymnastics and judo. Howell was an excellent all-around athlete who dedicated much of his time and energy to promoting health through lifelong physical activity. He believed skateboarding could be part of a healthy lifestyle.

Howell was born in September 1949, in Winston-Salem, North Carolina, but moved as a young child with his family to southern California. Beginning his competitive skateboarding career as a 25 year old, he was more mature than the typical teenage participant during the mid-1970s. Sponsors saw his maturity and supported him because they perceived him to be a good role model for their brands. In 1975, Howell and four other skaters, including Stacy Peralta, went to Australia for six months to promote skateboarding. In the mid-1970s, Howell had more than 150 different sponsors. His skills also helped him gain other work; he was a stunt actor in films, and made numerous appearances in surf and skateboard related films, as well as on television shows (Stevens, 2002).

Howell's belief that skateboarding can contribute to a healthy lifestyle led him to promote it as a mainstream sport, arguing that it should be incorporated into the Olympics and regular physical education curriculum (Mortimer, 2008). As another venue for promoting the value of skateboarding, he wrote three books on techniques and safety. His professional commitment to promoting physical activity was illustrated in earning a bachelor's degree in physical education in 1979.

As skateboarding took a cultural turn in the 1980s and became associated more with an urban punk lifestyle, Howell refocused his career on teaching computer science. In 1992, he moved from southern California to Boise, Idaho, where he continues to be an educator, web designer, and recreational skateboarder.

stacy peralta (1957–)

Peralta was a top skateboarder in the mid- to late 1970s. Although he essentially stopped skating professionally by 1980, his influence on skateboarding culture continued and has been profound. His innovations in promotions, primarily in videos and films, helped shape skateboarding culture by clearly marking it as antiestablishment and as an alternative to mainstream sport. He helped form the famous Bones Brigade of the 1980s, which initiated the business video trade, and he directed the 2001 award-winning documentary *Dogtown and Z Boys*.

Peralta was born October 15, 1957, in the Los Angeles area. His parents gave him a lot of freedom. which allowed him to explore his interests. One of those interests became a lifelong passion: surfing. As a young teenager, he spent most of his free time immersed in the surfing scene. During this time, he hung out at the Zephyr surf shop that eventually sponsored him as a surfer and skater (Brisick, 2010; Libes, 2003). Although he had recreationally skateboarded, it was his connection with the Zephyr surfers that helped him develop into a world-class skateboarder. In this group were owners Jeff Ho and Skip Engblom as well as artist, writer, and surfer Craig Stecyk. The young surfers also included Tony Alva and Jay Adams. Alva thought it would be a good idea to have Zephyr sponsor a skateboarding team, which came to be known as the Z-Boys. The team entered competitions and challenged many of the stylistic traditions of that time, creating commotion and getting publicity (Brooke, 1999). The Z-Boys team didn't last long, but it launched the careers of several of its members, including Peralta.

During the mid- to late 1970s, Peralta was on the top of the skateboarding world, and he embraced the opportunities for media coverage and international travel offered by his skateboarding success. When Peralta was 17 years old, Russ Howell invited him to go on a promotion tour to Australia for six months. He also did exhibitions in New Zealand and the Virgin Islands. He was featured in skateboarding magazines. He starred in the 1976 movie *Freewheelin'*. He had several sponsors and a best-selling signature board. In 1979, he had a role as a skateboarding kid on the popular TV drama *Charlie's Angels*. In 1980, he starred in the movie *Skateboard Madness*.

It was his decision to become business partners with George Powell that altered how Peralta would contribute to skateboarding. Their company was called Powell Peralta, and Stacy was involved in promotions. The strategy to increase the visibility of skateboarding companies was to sponsor a group of skaters (calling them a team) and have them tour doing demonstrations. Peralta had an eye for identifying unique talent. He faced what everyone else in the industry did, the early 1980s decline in the popularity of skateboarding. He had several strategies, but the most apparent one is his development of skateboarding videos. He developed the concept of telling a story, adding humor, and highlighting the personalities of the sponsored skaters as a central part of the videos. The Bones Brigade was the name of the Powell Peralta team, and a series of videos about the team was made throughout the 1980s. These were immensely popular and have set the standard for the industry (Dinces, 2011).

Peralta acknowledged that the downturn of the early 1980s changed his perspective on how to market and promote skateboarding. In the mid-1970s, he wanted skateboarding to go mainstream, but when he became more directly involved in the business side, he felt that skateboarding needed to develop an identity that differed from surfing and mainstream sports (Mortimer, 2008). Peralta acknowledges creating an urban feel to differentiate skateboarding from surfing and promoting a do-it-yourself (DIY) culture that differentiated from the mainstream. He and Fausto Vitello, the editor of *Thrasher* magazine, started to promote "street" skateboarding in the 1980s as a means to increase sales. They thought that vert skating had too limited a demographic and believed that street-style skateboarding would be accessible to more people and thus create more opportunities for involvement. The desire to broaden the skateboarding market led to creating a different style and identity, one that was urban, street, and antiauthoritarian (Greenfeld, 2004; Mortimer, 2008).

Powell Peralta became one of the top skateboarding companies in the 1980s. During this time, Peralta was making connections in Hollywood, consulting with directors who were incorporating skateboarding into films, such as the movie *Gleaming the Cube*. In 1991, Peralta decided to leave Powell Peralta and concentrate on becoming a screenplay writer and director. He had several jobs throughout the 1990s, but his big break came when he directed the documentary on the Z-Boys. The movie garnered critical acclaim. He has continued making documentaries, including one on big wave surfing, *Riding Giants*, and another on gangs in Los Angeles, *Crips and Bloods: Made in America*.

laura thornhill caswell (1961–)

Laura Thornhill was one of the top female skateboarders in the 1970s. She was known for her tenacity and versatility. Her preferred styles of participation were freestyle, vert in pools, and in the Arizona pipes as well as slalom on the steep hills of Mt. Baldy in southern California. Her skill brought her recognition; she was the first female to have a full-length profile in *Skateboarder* magazine and first woman to have a signature board (O'Mahoney, n.d.).

Thornhill was born in Dallas, Texas, on March 23, 1961. As a youngster in Texas, she was active in a variety of sports and experimented with skateboarding. In January 1974, her family moved to a city in southern California, Redondo Beach. Two months later, she received a skateboard for her birthday and quickly became engrossed. She connected with boys with whom she practiced and then beat them all at a local contest held at her middle school. Her big break was at the Steve's South Bay contest in 1975. She won both the freestyle and slalom events. A representative from Logan Earth Ski asked her to join their team. Within a year and a half, she had a signature board from Logan (O'Mahoney, n.d.; Thornhill, 2009).

In 1978, she switched teams and rode for Free Former. One of her first demonstrations with them was at an outdoor concert called the Cal Jam II. She and two other team members performed on stage in front of 350,000 people. They used a plexiglass half pipe (which allowed spectators a better view) and a wooden ramp as part of their demonstration.

In the late 1970s, a series of injuries caused her to retire from skateboarding. She still skates but not competitively. Instead, her competitive drive has been expressed in both street and mountain bike races, and she is active in snowboarding and yoga. She married in 1987 and has two children, Sage and Kylie (O'Mahoney, n.d.; Thornhill, 2009).

duane peters (1961–)

Duane Peters epitomized the punk rock skateboarder of the 1980s. A talented pool skater with an aggressive style, Peters was often referred to as the "master of disaster." He also served as a conduit for the punk rock and skateboard subcultures. Today, he still embodies this connection as he continues to skate and perform music.

Peters was born on June 12, 1961, in Anaheim, California. His mother suggests that Duane was a risktaker from an early age. As a young boy, he would play "chicken" by seeing how close he could get to cars or trains without being hit (Lucero, 2005). His parents divorced when he was nine, shifting the family landscape. Initially, he and his siblings lived with their mom in near poverty. At 13, Duane was living with his dad in Newport Beach, a situation that did not change his risktaking behavior; instead, he further challenged authority by skipping school and ultimately dropping out (Kane, 2010; Lucero, 2005). He started seriously skating pools and at that point embodied the southern California surfer, sporting surf apparel and long blonde hair. His Orange County skate crew called itself Thai L Stix (MacKaye, n.d.; Lucero, 2005). Thai Sticks is a reference to marijuana, which foreshadowed much of Peters's adult life.

Peters built his reputation on his aggressive and fearless style. One incident that secured this reputation when he was 16 were his attempts and success at completing a loop, skating 360 degrees in a full pipe. In the process, he broke his collarbone, but that was also a badge of courage. Attempting the loop was part of his audition for an arena laser-light entertainment show called *Skateboardmania*. Peters went on to be involved in this show, which featured skateboarders performing a drama that set earthlings against space invaders. Although the show did not garner much respect from the skateboarding community, it did provide its participants with a paycheck (MacKaye, n.d.; Lucero, 2005).

Peters was sponsored by Hobie, traveled locally with his team, and did demonstrations. He was also getting heavily involved in alcohol and drugs. In 1978 while he was drunk, he fell down a flight of stairs and shattered his elbow. The damage was so extensive that he was in the hospital for three months (Lucero, 2005). His return to skateboarding was successful, and he began to fully embrace his punk rock persona. He donned a crew cut and displayed swastikas on his body and car. He was known for an antiestablishment attitude, which included spitting at his competitors. Yet this attitude and his talent won him respect among some groups of young skateboarders, which appealed to some industry members. Recognizing the appeal of this rebellious and reckless image, Santa Cruz skateboards created a punk team by sponsoring Peters and two others: Steve Olson and Steve Alba, who is known as Salba. Peters was at the top of his career in the early 1980s, right when skateboarding's popularity declined. His last competition was in 1982, a contest that he lost to a young Tony Hawk.

Peters's commitment to punk rock became his primary focus after 1982. He lived in San Francisco playing music and skating with a crew called the Jax. He met a woman with whom he had two children, but their drug addiction and conviction on a theft charge led to her grandparents attaining custody of their children (Lucero, 2005).

Peters moved back to southern California and during the 1990s was on the road for eight years with different bands, winning most acclaim with the U.S. Bombs. Peters met his new partner, Corey Parks, through music. She's a bass player in the band the Hunns. They had a child together, Clash, in 2004.

In the 2000s, old-school skateboarding became hip again, and the industry supported it by creating pool contests with "masters" or "legends" divisions. Duane Peters has participated in these events, and he continues to create and play music today.

rodney mullen (1966–)

Mullen dominated freestyle skating throughout the 1980s, winning 36 of 37 competitions. But in the early 1990s, he shifted to street style. He developed many freestyle tricks, including several variations of the ollie and kickflip, that have become standard components of today's street style. His creative repertoire provided a crucial foundation as he took traditional flatland moves and adapted them for the various terrains of the street. Additionally, he has been involved in the industry first as a co-owner with Steve Rocco of World Industries; more recently, he started Almost Skateboards with Daewon Song.

Rodney Mullen was born in Gainesville, Florida, on August 17, 1966. He initially became interested in skateboarding through his sister's friends who were part of the alternative surfing crowd. His father was a former military man and a practicing dentist. He was strict, didn't want Rodney associating with the countercultural skateboarders and surfers, and initially forbade him from skating. But a deal was struck in the Mullen household on New Year's Eve 1976. That evening, his father had a few drinks and Rodney persuaded him to let him skate. Dr. Mullen agreed but required Rodney to wear protective equipment; if Rodney were injured, he must quit (Brooke, 1999; McReynolds, 2008; Mortimer, 2008; "Bio," n.d.).

Mullen quickly became successful. He was sponsored by a local Florida shop nine months after he started skateboarding and in 1979 won a contest in Oceanside, California. Stacy Peralta invited him to his first professional contest in San Diego in 1980. He was 13 years old and beat Steve Rocco to win. Because of this performance, Peralta invited him to be on the Bones Brigade team. Throughout the 1980s, Mullen was featured in several of the Bones Brigade videos and had a part in the mainstream movie *Gleaming the Cube* (Brooke, 1999; Mortimer, 2008). He also had a regular column with *Thrasher* magazine that provided tips on how to perform tricks.

As the 1980s were coming to an end, so was the popularity of freestyle. Steve Rocco and Mike Ternasky of Plan B encouraged Mullen to start shifting to street style, which he did. The 1990s ushered in a new chapter in Mullen's career. In addition to shifting his skating style, he and Steve Rocco started what turned out to be one of the largest skateboard companies, World Industries (Brooke, 1999; Mortimer, 2008). Throughout the 1990s, he was actively involved in the industry as both an owner and a skater (for several different sponsors). In 2001, World Industries was sold for $46 million to Globe, where Mullen continued on in a management position ("Bio," n.d.). A year later, he started his own company with Daewon Song called Almost Skateboards.

His popularity and reputation are as solid now as they were in the 1980s. In 2002, he won *Transworld Skateboading*'s readers' choice award for skater of the year. He continues to be featured in skateboard media, including his avatar in many of Tony Hawk's video games. Mullen has reflected on his career and commented that during the 1980s, he was overly concerned about winning, which took away from his enjoyment of the activity. He still skates daily but now prefers to skate alone so that he can skate for himself and the sheer pleasure of the activity (McReynolds, 2008; Mortimer, 2008).

patty segovia-krause (1966–)

Patty Segovia-Krause has played a significant role in promoting and legitimizing females in skateboarding. She developed and runs the All Girl Skate Jam, has authored or coauthored three books on females in skateboarding, serves as an agent for many professional female skateboarders, and is a professional photographer whose material focuses on females in skateboarding and snowboarding. Her combined efforts have helped put girls and women on the skateboarding map.

As a southern California youngster in the 1970s, Patty was exposed to the thriving skateboarding scene. Her cousin Tony Rock Jetton was a pro in the 1970s and was an inspiration to Patty. She was born in March 1966, grew up in a town called South Gate, and attended St. Pius X High School in Downey. Her father bought her a plastic board when she was 12 years old; when she started to get hurt, he took her board away. Nonetheless, Patty kept at it. When visiting her cousin Tony, she would jump at the opportunity to ride his board but had to hide this from her parents or they would have stopped her. She skated with a group of friends known as Team Un, which consisted of mainly males but did occasionally include one other female. Segovia-Krause graduated from high school in 1984 and continued her involvement in the underground skate/punk scene in Los Angeles. She skated with her friends and listened to the musical punk bands Suicidal Tendencies and Social Distortion while practicing in garages.

Segovia-Krause also learned to snowboard. She associated with a group of women who would travel the East and West Coasts of the United States and Canada skating and snowboarding. Her career in photography was inspired during her involvement with this group. She started photographing her friends to document their scene but then quickly developed her skill, and her photos were published. Patty attended University of California— Santa Barbara, lived in the same apartment complex as students who attended a local arts school, the Brooke Institute, and acquired great technical tips for her photography. Segovia-Krause knew that women needed more opportunities in contests and in media coverage to help develop their interests and talents. This knowledge encouraged not only her career in photography, but also a career in recruiting skateboarding-specific as well as other corporate sponsorship for her contests. In 1990, in Reno, Nevada, Patty set up the first All Girls Skate Jam, in which five females participated. Segovia-Krause participated and placed third. Cara-Beth Burnside won the event; pro skater Danny Way was one of the judges at the age of 16.

In 1996, Patty earned a bachelor's degree in sociology from University of California–Santa Barbara. The next year, she institutionalized the All Girl Skate Jam (AGSJ), a skateboard competition for females of all skill levels and ages. Since 1997 the contest has been held annually. The AGSJ provides media attention, sponsorship, and networking for females. In addition, the AGSJ runs camps and works with other community groups to provide skateboarding lessons for girls. The AGSJ contests are held throughout the United States and a few other countries. In 2003, AGSJ competitions were incorporated into Vans' Warped Tour, providing females with more exposure. Segovia-Krause created the nonprofit International Girl Skateboarding Association (IGSA) in 1999 to extend support globally. She continues her work with other skateboarding entities and various types of media to provide more competitive opportunities and media coverage for females. Currently, she is a producer for the *Skater Girls* national reality TV show (personal interview with Segovia-Krause, August 20, 2009).

christian hosoi (1967–)

Hosoi was one of the best skaters of the 1980s, admired for his beautifully flowing style and ability to get big air. His signature tricks were the Christ Air and Rocket Air. Tony Hawk and Hosoi were top contenders and rivals throughout a majority of the 1980s. Hosoi was also known for his generosity and his Hollywood lifestyle because he socialized and partied with actors and musicians.

Hosoi was born in October 5, 1967, in Hawaii. As a young child, he moved to the Los Angeles area with his father. Influenced by his father, Ivan, an underemployed artist who ran a southern California skate park, Hosoi started skating at an early age (Greenfeld, 2004; Freedman & Montano, 2006). He had the support of some of the well-known Dogtown skaters such as Tony Alva and Stacey Peralta, and his main role model was Shogu Kubo. He became sponsored by Powell Peralta at the age of 14; earning nearly $1,000 a month, he dropped out of high school (Yoshiura, n.d.). A year later, he switched to be a part of Dogtown skates (Tony Alva's brand). His status rose rapidly in the early 1980s, as he was one of the most dynamic vertical skaters. He cultivated an artistic style, often skating shirtless or wearing neon colors and spandex shorts (Freedman & Montano, 2006). In addition, he changed his hair style and color frequently. His skill and dramatic style appealed to those outside of skateboarding; he was the epitome of youthful cool and was commonly referred to as the rock star of skateboarding. Hosoi appeared in the Beastie Boys' music video "Pass the Mic," and he associated with the band members of the Red Hot Chili Peppers. In addition to skateboarding companies, other apparel companies recognized the economic potential of Hosoi's popularity and offered him lucrative sponsorship deals. But at the age of 17, an entrepreneurial Hosoi decided to capitalize on his skills and cultural status, founding his own company, Hosoi Skates, which manufactured his signature hammerhead skateboard (Greenfeld, 2004, Yoshiura, n.d.). In the late 1980s, he was earning hundreds of thousands of dollars a year from contests, sponsorship deals, and his own brand, Hosoi Skates. In 1987, he and Louann Rawls, his girlfriend at the time, moved into W. C. Fields's old house in Los Angeles and built a ramp in the backyard (Greenfeld, 2004).

His career and life were altered with the collapse of skateboarding's popularity in the early 1990s, which negatively affected his skateboarding business ventures and led to less opportunity for Hosoi to compete professionally. This time period also saw the shift from emphasizing vertical to emphasizing street style, which also reduced the demand for Hosoi's talents. It was during this time that Hosoi became deeply involved in illicit drugs; especially punishing was his addiction to crystal methamphetamine (meth). All these factors came together to form the perfect storm. When his girlfriend left him in 1991 and he was forced to move out of his mother's home, he moved to Orange County (Greenfeld, 2004). In 1995, he was charged with possession of drug paraphernalia. He skipped his hearing, and a warrant was issued for his arrest. Hosoi had to go underground, which meant giving up public skateboarding appearances, including the first X Games (then called the Extreme Games). The producers wanted to rekindle the rivalry between Hosoi and Hawk, but Hosoi didn't show up. Some have speculated that if Hosoi had participated in the first X Games, he may have become a household name much like Hawk, or perhaps instead of Hawk (Greenfeld, 2004; Yoshiura, n.d.).

In 2000, he was arrested in Hawaii for carrying a pound and a half of crystal methamphetamine. He served four years and then was released. During his prison time, he converted to Christianity. In 2005, he became an ordained minister and is a pastor at the Sanctuary church in Huntington Beach, California (Freedman & Montano, 2006). He has revived his skateboarding career by competing in masters divisions and building a ministry called *The Uprising* that was developed into a reality TV program.

tony hawk (1968–)

Tony Hawk has become the public face of skateboarding. He has the biggest name recognition of any sport star for young consumers (Iwata, 2008). He is known for his skills in vert, his innovative tricks, and his personal drive. He has created between 85 and 150 tricks such as the stalefish, airwalk, and Madonna (Browne, 2004). And, unlike many of his counterparts, he has a clean-cut image: no visible tattoos, short cropped hair, and an unassuming demeanor. This makes him appealing to a broad audience. His remarkable skateboarding skills, business savvy, and wholesome image have made him an icon (Hyman, 2006).

Hawk was born on May 12, 1968, in the San Diego area. He was a self-proclaimed hyper kid who had trouble fitting into traditional youth activities. He tried many organized sports, including basketball and baseball, but then quit. He got into skateboarding and created an identity through that, eschewing traditional high school activities. His older brother Steve was a surfer and introduced Tony to skating at an early age (Levine, 1999). Tony started to skate on a regular basis when he was nine. He entered his first competition when he was 11.

His father, Frank Hawk, was supportive. Even though Frank was the president of the Little League organization that Tony played in for a few years, Frank created institutional support for his son's growing interest and passion in skateboarding. Frank Hawk started the California Amateur Skateboard League and then the National Skateboard Association in 1983 (Layden, 2002).

In 1982, Stacy Peralta recruited the 14-year-old Hawk to ride for Powell Peralta. He became part of the legendary Bones Brigade (the name of the sponsored team) and was given a signature board. The Bones Brigade was legendary not only because of their skill, but because of the videos that revolutionized the video market and created skateboarding stars of its members. In addition, Hawk was one of the best vert skaters in the 1980s, winning nearly every competition he entered. He was so popular that in the mid- to late 1980s, he was earning over $100,000 a year (Browne, 2004).

The downturn in the popularity of skateboarding during the early 1990s negatively affected Hawk's career prospects and income. As well as the downturn in the skateboarding market many skateboarders were also shifting their attention and energies away from vert and toward street skating. Recognizing these economic and cultural shifts, Hawk invested in his first skateboarding business, Birdhouse, in 1992. Hawk's luck changed in 1995 when ESPN created the Extreme Games (later called the X Games) and included vert skateboarding as a key event. Hawk accepted the invitation to compete; he went on to win the vert competition and placed second in the street (Layden, 2002). The media coverage of Hawk's performances, and the sport more broadly, helped boost the industry once again. Hawk continued to skate in competitions and demonstrations throughout the 1990s. In 1999, he secured his name in history, becoming the first person to successfully land a difficult trick, the 900, at the X Games.

This is also the period when his name and image recognition was successfully managed by his sister Pat Hawk. In 1998, he started Tony Hawk, Inc., which includes five divisions: merchandising, endorsements, events, films, and digital media. Hawk Clothing was created in 1998; two years later, he sold it to Quiksilver, one of the largest global surf and action sports corporations. In 1999, he worked with video game producer Activision to create Tony Hawk Pro Skater. The game was a top seller. Every year since, Activision has put out different versions of the video game. In 2001, it was the seventh biggest seller out of all video games (Layden, 2002). These games feature other skateboarders as well; it is often a sign of celebrity status when one's avatar is used in a Tony Hawk game.

Hawk also created a series of traveling skateboard demonstrations, The Gigantic Skatepark Tour, that was filmed for a show on ESPN. This transformed into the Boom Boom Huck Jam, a choreographed skateboard, BMX bike, and motocross athletes performing together accompanied by live punk bands, they performed at amusement parks. Six Flags has a roller coaster called Tony Hawk's Big Spin and a waterslide that emulates the experience of a half pipe (Rubial, 2008).

Hawk also has created media outlets as well. He owns a film production studio, 900 Films, and a network called Funny or Die. In addition, he hosts a show, *Tony Hawk's Demolition Show*, on Sirius Radio. Hawk has parlayed his skateboarding image into a variety of businesses, and today he is a multimillionaire (Iwata, 2008). He has a foundation that provides resources to build skateparks in low-income neighborhoods; as of 2010, the foundation has help build 425 parks.

Hawk has been married and divorced three times, and he has a daughter (Kadance) and three sons (Riley, Spencer, and Keegan) from those marriages. He currently lives in southern California.

cara-beth burnside (1968–)

Cara-Beth Burnside is one of the most accomplished skateboarders, winning over 16 titles, and she has been a significant role model for contemporary female skaters. Cara-Beth, often referred to as CB, played a pivotal role in gaining acceptance for female skateboarders in the 1990s and today. She weathered the lean times for women in the 1980s, as there was little support from the industry, but her continued efforts paid off as she became highly respected and helped to usher in a new era for females. Burnside has parlayed her skateboarding skills to being a spokesperson for females in the sport as well as environmental causes.

Burnside was born in Orange, California, on July 23, 1968. She spent much of her free time outdoors riding her pony, BMX bike, and motorcycle (Norcross, 2006). She became interested in skateboarding during its boom in the mid-1970s. Her parents were supportive of her newfound passion. Burnside has noted that skateboarders Patty Hoffman, Duane Peters, and Tony Alva also provided inspiration and encouragement (Owen, 2000). Cara-Beth was winning competitions at the age of 12, but the popularity of skateboarding took a downturn at this time, so her achievements gained little attention outside of her immediate peer group. Therefore, Cara-Beth put skateboarding on the back burner while she finished high school (Egan, 1998). She refocused her athletic pursuits on karate, where she earned a brown belt, and soccer, which she played at the collegiate level. She attended the University of California–Davis and earned a degree in human development (Corbett, 2000).

In the late 1980s, she again began to pursue skateboarding, and her skill was acknowledged when *Thrasher* magazine put her on its cover in August 1989. To compete as a professional, she started her own company and created her own signature board. There were no female-only competitions, so she competed against men (Egan, 1998). Even though she proved her skills, she became discouraged from lack of support and in the early 1990s gravitated toward snowboarding, as that culture was more welcoming of females. By the mid-1990s, she was one of the top snowboarders in the world, placing fourth in the half pipe at the 1998 winter Olympics (Corbett, 2000).

Although snowboarding offered more opportunities for female athletes during this period, Burnside continued to develop her skateboarding skills alongside her snowboarding career. With the advent of the All Girls Skate Jam and other concerted efforts to promote female skateboarding, Burnside became one of the top skaters. Juggling successful careers in both skateboarding and snowboarding, she has won gold medals in both the winter and summer X Games, Vans Triple Crown, and All Girl Skate Jam. *Transworld* magazine named her the top female skateboarder of the year in 2003, and one organizing body, World Cup Skateboarding, recognized her as the Female Vert Skater of the Year in 2004. In snowboarding culture, Burnside had been gaining considerable media coverage and sponsorship deals for a number of years; it wasn't until later that the skateboarding industry began to recognize her skills such that she increasingly gained the attention of skateboarding media and sponsors. Burnside was also a strong advocate for the rights of female skateboarders, and she fought to negotiate space for women practicing the sport or working in the industry. As a result of her skills and advocacy, she was the first female skateboarder to have a signature shoe (with Vans) and a flexdeck signature board; in addition, she was sponsored by various clothing and equipment companies. Like many other skaters and snowboarders, Burnside's accomplishments came at some physical cost. She has endured five concussions and a broken collarbone ("Cara-Beth Burnside," n.d.).

Throughout the first decade of the 2000s, she continued to work on behalf of female skateboarders. In 2005, she and other skaters created the Alliance, an advocacy group for female skaters. One of the group's main accomplishments was to negotiate with ESPN for equal prize money for women and men skateboarders in the 2009 X Games. Burnside also actively supports environmental causes; she is one of the cofounders of the Action Sports Environmental Coalition.

danny way (1974–)

Danny Way is known for his creativity and courage, as exemplified by his desire and ability to ride a skateboard fast and to jump it as far and high as possible. He is the creator of the MegaRamp, which became included in the X Games as a regular event. He also used it to jump the Great Wall of China in July 2005. He has been named Skateboarder of the Year twice by the skate magazine *Thrasher*.

Way was born on April 15, 1974, in Portland, Oregon, although he grew up primarily in San Diego. Way's childhood was turbulent. His father died when he was eight months old, and soon after his mother, Mary, started abusing drugs and socializing with some problematic people. She remarried a man named Tim O'Dea, which brought some stability to the family. O'Dea introduced Danny and his brother Damon to surfing and skateboarding.

Skateboarder Danny Way catches air as he performs at Hard Rock Hotel-Casino in Las Vegas on April 6, 2006. Earlier, Way successfully dropped off the Hard Rock Hotel guitar sign during his practice, 28 feet above a 56-foot-high ramp, in an attempt to set a Guinness world record for the highest bomb-drop. (AP Photo/Jae C. Hong)

A few years later, O'Dea left the family, and Way's mother returned to using drugs and being involved in abusive relationships. Way talks about how he used skateboarding as therapy. Way's youthful personality was shaped by living in continuous chaos and abuse, and he was known to be brash, but his skill spoke volumes. He was sponsored by Powell Peralta in the 1980s and later turned professional with a contract with H-Street in 1989. At this time, he was 15, winning contests, and collecting royalty checks nearing $20,000 a month (Johnston, 2010). Shortly thereafter, he quit that team and lost his edge. Then he was recruited to skate on Plan B when he was 17. He blossomed as part of this group. In 1993 Danny and a few of his friends, Colin McKay, Damon Way and Ken Block, started DC shoes which proved to be a boon a decade later when they sold their DC brand to surfing giant Quiksilver for $87 million (Daugherty, 2008). In 1994, Danny's mentor at Plan B, Mike Ternasky, was killed in a motor vehicle crash. Plan B closed in 1995. That year, Danny broke his neck while surfing. At 20 years of age, Way was partially paralyzed for a year. He beat the odds and was able to skate in 1996, when he came back as determined and courageous as ever.

During the next stage in his career, he started to increase the danger of his feats. In 1997, Way dropped 35 feet from a helicopter onto a vert ramp. It was also during the late 1990s that he started to experiment with building a MegaRamp. He built several versions in the California desert, keeping the project secret. He used a 2003 DC video to launch the MegaRamp to the public. In 2004, the X Games included the MegaRamp as a competitive event. In 2005, Way used a MegaRamp to jump the Great Wall of China. Way restarted the company, Plan B, in 2005 and recently partnered with another surfing giant, Billabong, to help promote and distribute his products. In 2007, he had a car tow him on his skateboard, clocking 75.4 mile per hour. In his career of pushing skateboarding's limits, he has also pushed his body's limits, enduring 13 major operations (Higgins, 2009).

Way was married to Kari for several years (the marriage ended in 2009), and they have three children: two sons, Ryden and Tavin, and a daughter, Rumi. Currently, he has a ranch on the Hawaiian island of Kuai, where he is planning another version of the MegaRamp (Johnston, 2010). He plays guitar in a band called Escalera with fellow skateboarder Bob Burnquist and three others.

rob dyrdek (1974–)

Dyrdek is a professional skateboarder but has made his mark as a consummate entrepreneur, continually developing ways to develop a broad audience for street-style skateboarding. He has done this in several ways. First, he has used skateboarding as a means to create and sell other forms of entertainment, such as action figures and television programs. Second, he has promoted the development of skate parks across the United States that feature street apparatus. Third, he has developed a professional skateboard league, which rewards skaters handsomely with the goal of becoming the premier competition series. Dyrdek has used his business skills to expand the cultural appeal of street skateboarding.

Dyrdek was born in Kettering, Ohio, on June 28, 1974. He started when he was 12 and quickly became successful. At 16, he turned professional and left high school. He moved to San Diego in 1994 to be closer to the skateboarding industry. When he was 21, he was sponsored by DC Shoes, which started a relationship in which he worked on shoe design and later created a joint venture for developing street skate parks, the Rob Dyrdek/DC Shoes Skate Plaza Foundation, which has built several parks across the United States. The first of these parks opened in 2005 in his hometown ("Rob Dyrdek Biography," n.d.).

Dyrdek's reach increased greatly with his partnership with MTV, where he has had two shows. *Rob and Big* aired from 2006 to 2008 and was about a skateboarder who hired a personal security guard to enable him to skate in public spaces. The second show started in 2009 and is called *Fantasy Factory*. It follows the development of various business ideas. He has used this show to promote his other ventures, including a successful toy line and a cartoon series about a group of friends who skateboard called Wild Grinders.

Dyrdek's interest in media led him to write and produce a film. In 2009, *Street Dreams*, a film about street skating, was released and featured the highly prominent skaters Paul Rodriguez, Jr., Ryan Sheckler, and Terry Kennedy. These athletes were also signed to his next business venture, the Street League.

Perhaps Dyrdek's most ambitious venture is creating a professional skateboarding league. In 2010, the Street League debuted. It featured street-style skateboarding that has the largest financial payout and provides revenue sharing for the athletes who compete. While it rewards the street skateboarders well, it also required them to sign a contract that does not allow them to compete in the three biggest competitions, the Maloof Money Cup, the Dew Tour, and the X Games. In this way, Dyrdek was trying to create the most prestigious tour. In addition, this tour was connected with his foundation, which would provide $50,000 to build skate plazas in the towns that host the competition (Wilson, 2010).

Rob Dyrdek is one of the most successful skateboarder/entrepreneurs. He has worked hard at developing a market for street skating, which he has done by tapping into a young adult audience through media, especially MTV.

elissa steamer (1975–)

Elissa Steamer is one of the elite street skaters of the past two decades and was the first female to gain mainstream recognition; her avatar was the first female skater in Tony Hawk's video game series and was included for five years.

Steamer was born on July 31, 1975, in Fort Myers, Florida. She was an adventurous child and enjoyed being outdoors. Skateboarding became an ideal means for her to explore and play outside. She was exposed to skateboarding as a young child. She remembers being on a skateboard at five years of age; her father bought her first board, a free former, when she was seven. Steamer also rode BMX bikes, but when she was nine, she found skateboard allies in the neighborhood who encouraged her involvement. To this day, she is still good friends with one of those people, Tim Mott. Her parents supported her commitment; her dad got her a board each birthday and Christmas, and her mom drove her to competitions. She delved into the skate culture by reading the niche magazines and watching the videos. While she was growing up, Fort Myers did not have any public skateparks that included ramps on which to practice vert skills. Thus, she focused on street style and was strongly influenced by the styles of fellow street skateboarders Ray Barbee and Matt Hensley. Her commitment to skateboarding took hold when she was about 12 years of age.

When she was 19, she moved to southern California and immersed herself in the scene by living with other skaters and practicing daily. It was during her nine years in southern California that her professional career took off. She turned pro at 22 years of age when she was sponsored by the manufacturer Toy Machine. She had a signature board with them and was featured in their video series *Welcome to Hell*. Additionally, she had a signature shoe with Etnies.

Elissa Steamer competes in Skateboard Street Women's Finals during the X Games outside the Staples Center in Los Angeles, August 5, 2005. Steamer won the competition. (AP Photo/Jae C. Hong.)

Her dominance in women's street competitions started the first time World Cup Skateboarding had a women's division, which occurred at the Slam City Jam in Vancouver, British Columbia in 1998. Elissa won the event, and she won it the following year as well. Her performance in the X Games illustrates her competitive prowess; she has been a top-three finisher six times (the first X Games that included women's skateboarding divisions was in 2003). Her continued success and high regard are demonstrated through her more recent sponsors, including Zero and Nike. In 2010, Steamer was given a guest signature board from Krooked that featured graphics by Mark Gonzales, who is one of the most famous street skateboarders and a well-regarded artist. This is a tribute that Elissa treasures. In fact, it is these types of incidents, ones that acknowledge her contributions to skateboarding, that she finds even more gratifying than winning competitions. She currently lives in San Francisco, where she has taken up surfing and continues to skateboard (personal interview with Steamer, September 21, 2010).

bob burnquist (1976–)

Bob Burnquist is one of the most durable and accomplished skaters. He has been a professional skater since the early 1990s. He won *Thrasher*'s skater of the year in 1997, has been ranked first in the world for vert by World Cup Skateboarding, and consistently places at or near the top in most major competitions. He is one of just a handful of athletes to compete in every X Games, where he has won 19 medals. In 2010, he was inducted into the Skateboarding Hall of Fame. Known for his switch stance and technical abilities in ramp skating, he continues to develop his skills and creativity, especially in MegaRamp skateboarding.

Burnquist was born in Rio De Janeiro, Brazil, on October 10, 1976. His father is American and his mother Brazilian. Burnquist moved several times while he was growing up, mainly to different cities in Brazil such as São Paolo and Port Alegre, but he also spent a year in the San Francisco Bay area when he was four years old. Burnquist was an active child who was involved in soccer and baseball, but his stamina was limited by chronic asthma (Browne, 2004). He started skating when he was 10 years old. He recalls how a friend lost his soccer ball and to repay him, gave Bob his skateboard. By the time he was 11, his father had bought him his own ("All About," n.d.). Good fortune had it that there was a skate park in Burnquist's neighborhood, and he was soon practicing daily and consuming skateboarding media (Higgins, 2006, November 1). At 14, Burnquist won his first amateur contest in Brazil.

His big break came in 1994 when *Thrasher* sponsored a tour of professional skaters in Brazil. Fluent in both Portuguese and English, Burnquist volunteered to translate for the American skateboarders. The *Thrasher* group was impressed by his skateboarding skills, invited him to San Francisco, and connected him with a sponsor. That sponsor paid his way to the 1995 Slam City Jam in Vancouver, British Columbia, where he unexpectedly won the vert competition, which jump-started his career (Higgins, 2006, November 1; "All About," n.d.). Since then, he has become one of the most visible and successful skateboarders.

In 1999, Burnquist bought a ranch property in southern California, where he has used the space to create different types of ramps (Higgins, 2006, November 1). Over time, he has built one of the few permanent MegaRamps with a rail, a vert ramp bowl, a loop ramp, a corkscrew, and a full pipe. He is the first person to do a 900 on a MegaRamp. His loop has a retractable top, allowing him to ride and jump the gap while being upside down. Among many memorable runs, one of his most daring was using a MegaRamp to jump to a 40-foot rail grinding into a parachute jump that dropped 1,600 feet into the Grand Canyon. He missed the rail on the first attempt but was able to recover enough to have a successful jump and landing. He was completely successful on the second run.

Like many of his peers, Burnquist has ventured into businesses associated with skateboarding, including ZooBamboo Entertainment, which runs Skateboard.TV. He is also a founding member of the Action Sports Environmental Coalition. Additionally, he has pursued other interests such as running an organic farm and a restaurant, playing drums in a band, and being a licensed pilot and skydiver. He has done this while being a father to three children. Lotus is his first child from his former partner and pro skater, Jen O'Brien. He currently is married to Veronica Nachard Burnquist, with whom he has two daughters: Vitoria and Jasmyn.

stevie williams (1979–)

Williams is one of the top street skateboarders. He has also been the most successful African American skateboarder, creating a brand around "skurban" culture, the intersection of skateboarding and urban culture. In April 2010, *Ebony* magazine named him one of the top young entrepreneurs (Christian, 2010). He started and owns one of the largest skateboard companies, Dirty Ghetto Kids (DGK), and has branched into media as well.

Stevie Williams was born in December 1979. He grew up in North Philadelphia and started skating when he was 10. At that time, skating was not well supported in the African American community, and he often was mocked for doing a "white" sport. He would go to the acclaimed Love Park, where various ethnicities skated. Nonetheless, he was often taunted as a "dirty ghetto kid," which later he took on as his brand name. When he was 15, he was sponsored by Element. He then dropped out of high school and went to California to be closer to the skateboarding industry. Williams lived in San Francisco, where he was approached by a startup company. Taking their offer, he left Element, but the startup went out of business, leaving Stevie without an income. When he was 18, he went back to Philadelphia where pro skater Josh Kalis helped him get back on track (Holthouse, 2007).

In the late 1990s and early 2000s, his growing reputation as a highly skilled and creative skateboarder provided him another entrée into the industry. Some of his newfound popularity is illustrated by being sponsored by DC Shoes in 1999; the following year, he was given the opportunity to help design his own model of shoes. In addition, he was featured as an avatar in several of Tony Hawk's video games. Attempting to capitalize on his cultural status, Williams started his own company, DGK, in 2002. Two years later, he coordinated a huge deal with Reebok to cobrand DGK. Williams was the first skateboarder that Reebok sponsored, and that deal made Williams a millionaire.

Using his entrepreneurial acumen, he expanded his brand by developing outlets into other cultural avenues that focused on clothing and music. For example, he has worked with Don Cannon, a famous music producer, to open an urban lifestyle shop in Atlanta that sold street skateboarding-inspired fashion and music (Annobil, 2009). Williams also has another skateboard store in southern California. In addition, Williams has created a foundation, Educate to Skate, which places computer labs in inner-city schools. As a professional skateboarder, he is on the road frequently but resides part of the year in southern California and part of the year in Atlanta. He has two children: Brooklyn and Paris.

vanessa torres (1986–)

Vanessa Torres is one of the top street skaters of the past decade. Despite a tumultuous childhood and youth, Torres has continued to develop her skateboarding skills and is widely recognized as among the world's top female skateboarders. She won the inaugural park competition for women when the X Games first sponsored a women's division in skateboarding (2003), and she regularly performs well in other contests. Her skill has been acknowledged by having a signature board for Element, her avatar being used in a Tony Hawk video game, being included in two videos featuring top women skateboarders, and a featured interview in *Thrasher* magazine.

Vanessa was born in July 1986 in the southern California city of Anaheim. Her parents were young teenagers, so she grew up in her maternal grandmother's house, receiving support from both her mother and grandmother. An active child, Vanessa was involved in various sports. In 1997, her family was living in Riverside, a southern California town located inland, when she received her first skateboard. A vibrant skate scene in a more coastal town captivated Vanessa, and she made her way to Irvine as much as possible. She met the mother of another skater who became her advocate and connected her to people in the industry, including the owner of a local southern California skate shop who offered Vanessa her first sponsorship. Her advocate also took her to the All Girls Skate Jam in San Diego in 2000, where 14-year-old Vanessa went on to win the competition. Her performance gained the attention of many within the skateboarding industry, including her first shoe sponsor (Zitzer, 2010). Soon after, she was skating in contests against some of the top female skaters, including Elissa Steamer and Jamie Reyes.

Her burgeoning skating career was disrupted when her mother and stepfather moved to a town in central California, hundreds of miles north. Disconnected from the vibrant skate scene and her grandmother, Vanessa struggled to transition to the central California town of Modesto, and her relationship with her mother became strained. Her discontentedness was evidenced in many ways. For example, the skateboarding company Element invited Vanessa to a training camp. Instead of waiting for her mother to pick her up afterward, she took the Element van that headed to southern California without notifying her mother (Zitzer, 2010).

Even though her home life was tense, Vanessa continued to invest her energies into developing her skating skills. She and a few other women, including Amy Caron and Jamie Reyes, were chosen to be in a video that was shot in Australia, *AKA: Skater Girl*. Two years later, Vanessa was in another video featuring many top women, including Lyn-Z Adams Hawkins and Cara-Beth Burnside, *Getting Nowhere Faster*. In 2005, she moved to southern California, where she did well in competitions and which she used as a base as she began to travel the world. During this period, however, she became distracted by the party lifestyle, which took a toll on her career such that she decided to move back to Modesto to live with her family. After reprioritizing her goals, she moved back to southern California, where she continues to skateboard successfully (Zitzer, 2010).

lyn-z adams hawkins pastrana (1989–)

Adams Hawkins Pastrana is one of the best currently practicing female vert skateboarders, although she is also highly skilled in street and bowl. She is the first female to land a 540 McTwist, a difficult trick, and the first female to successfully jump the MegaRramp, which is nine stories tall and has a 55-foot gap as well as a 28-foot quarter pipe landing. Her avatar has been featured in three of Tony Hawk's video games.

Adams Hawkins Pastrana was born on September 21, 1989, in the San Diego area. When she was nine years old, she started spelling her given

Lyn-Z Adams Hawkins catches air during the Skateboard Vert Women's Final at the X Games, August 2, 2008, in Los Angeles. Adams Hawkins took second in the event. (AP Photo/Mark J. Terrill)

name Lindsey as Lyn-Z, and with her parents' consent, her version became permanent. She grew up with a physically active family that fostered and supported her passion for skateboarding. Her parents bought her a skateboard before she was two years old, and her brother gave her a membership to the local skate park when she was six. She also participated in soccer, baseball, basketball, swimming, diving, and gymnastics (Lannes, 2010, January 19). She continues to surf and snowboard. She became involved in competitive skateboarding in 2000, at the age of 11, when she competed in the All Girls Skate Jam. It was there that she recognized that there was a future for females in skateboarding. During the next two years, she traveled to several top-notch amateur competitions, where she did well ("Lyn-Z Adams Hawkins," n.d.).

In 2003, at the age of 14, she competed in the first ever women's skateboard competitions featured in the X Games, where she earned a silver medal in the street contest and a bronze in the vert contest. The next year, she won gold in the women's vert. Since then, she won either silver or gold in the vert when she competed in the X Games.

During her teenage years, she had a series of setbacks. Her father, who had always been a great support to her, died in December 2003, and then she endured several injures. In 2005, she broke her arm; in 2006, a snowboarding accident tore her anterior cruciate ligament (ACL) ("Lyn-Z Adams Hawkins," n.d.). This injury forced her to take a year off from competition. But she came back to win a gold medal in the vert event at the 2007 X Games, which she repeated in 2009. She gained a silver in 2010. She further solidified her status as one of the world's most courageous and skilled female skateboarders when she successfully performed the first 540 McTwist at the Quiksilver Tony Hawk Show in Paris (France) in 2009 and was one of the few skateboarders, and the first female, to jump the infamous DC MegaRamp. Adams Hawkins also has toured with Nitro Circus Live, a tour of top talent in a variety of extreme sports, including skateboarding, BMX, and motocross. In October 2011, Adams Hawkins married one of the top extreme sport athletes in motocross and founder of Nitro Circus Live, Travis Pastrana.

Adams Hawkins continues to live in the San Diego area practicing with top male and female vert skaters, including Tony Hawk and Cara-Beth Burnside. She is a member of the Action Sports Environmental Coalition and serves on the athlete advisory panel for the Woman's Sports Foundation.

nyjah huston (1994–)

Nyjah Huston is one of the best of the younger generation of skaters. He is known as one of the most consistent performers in street skateboarding. He won the most prestigious American amateur competition, Tampa

Nyjah Huston competes in the Skateboard Street Final during the X Games at the Home Depot Center in Carson, California, August 1, 2009. Huston took second place. (AP Photo/Lori Shepler)

Am, when he was 10 years old. In 2006, when he was 11, he competed in the X Games and still holds the record as the youngest person to participate in the X Games. At the end of 2006, World Cup Skateboarding ranked him the seventeenth best street skater in the world. Since then, he has placed consistently in X Games, Street League, and Maloof Money Cup competitions. In 2011, at the age of 17, his competition earnings topped $600,000. In addition to his brilliant skills, Nyjah's trademark was his long dreadlocks. At 16 years of age, he cut his hair short and altered his relationship with his dominant father.

Nyjah was born on November 30, 1994. He has three brothers and one sister. His family lives in Davis, California, which is located between San Francisco and Sacramento. His father, Adeyemi, was a skateboarder and managed Nyjah's career. His management style became domineering as he controlled Nyjah's training and money. Nyjah said, "My dad was always [a] really controlling, protective person. He always wanted me to stay really focused and not get into partying or girls or anything. I'd say it affected my social life" (in Nieratko, 2011). His father bought land in Puerto Rico and started a skateboard company called I & I, where he lost all of Nyjah's money (Nieratko, 2011, 75). "Ever since I was 11, I was making pretty good money. I never gave a thought about money. By the time I was 15, it was pretty much all gone," Nyjah said (in Nieratko, 2011, 72).

When Nyjah turned 16, he made a break from his father and started living with his mother, Kelle Huston. "But now I can think for myself and I have so much more freedom and so much more fun now laughing with everyone," he said (in Nieratko, 2011, 75). He has reestablished relations with his original sponsor, Element, and is now riding on their team. Even with his newfound freedom, Nyjah is still performing at a high level. In 2011, he placed second in Tampa Pro, had a second overall finish in Street League, and earned a gold medal in the X Games.

more voices

The 19 people featured in this chapter are influential members of the skateboarding community. Needless to say, it is difficult to limit a discussion of prominent figures to just one chapter. Additionally, a major ethos of the skateboarding community is to celebrate all who participate and to respect the meaning and value skateboarding provides to each. An important complement to this chapter is a book called *Lives on Board* (2009), which provides stories from over 100 people, each of whom writes about the impact skateboarding has made on his or her life.

5. navigating the built environment: technology and physics

skateboarding is fundamentally about using technology to transverse human-made environments. There is no "back to nature" sentiment or desire to find oneself by engaging the "natural" world. Instead, skateboarding is about navigating and redefining the human-built environment (Borden, 2001; Davidson, 1985). Thus, skateboarding is a technological *and* artistic response to urbanization (see Chapter 3, "Venues for Creativity"). Crucial to the progression and variation in skateboarding skills and styles have been enhancements in technology related to equipment, ramps, and other elements central to the activity.

While the actual form of the skateboard hasn't changed much, the materials and modifications have led to improved board performance. Additionally, design improvements have been made to pools, ramps, and other elements used by skateboarders. These improvements have led to progressive performance styles and maneuvers that can be explained by physics, especially the physical laws of motion. Finally, technological advances in media have provided greater educational and social avenues for skaters to display, distribute, and discuss their skills.

equipment and technology

The essential piece of equipment used by skateboarders is the skateboard, which has three basic components: the deck, the trucks (axle), and the wheels. As skateboarders have experimented to find a smoother, faster, and more maneuverable ride, the materials and design of the components have changed over time. The first skateboards were solid pieces of wood with roller skate trucks and metal wheels attached. Although the basic design of the trucks has changed little, the board and wheels have. Wheels evolved from metal to clay, to polyurethane. The board has gone from a single piece of oak to seven layers of maple, and versions that have included fiberglass, aluminum, and plastic. The 1970s saw the greatest experimentation with materials for the board, and the 1970s and 1980s witnesses a wide variation in the size and shape of boards, some of it due to marketing ploys and some due to sincere design improvement. One of the best-known marketing designs was Christian Hosoi's hammerhead board, which had a nose shaped like a hammerhead shark. This design feature was solely to differentiate the board and was not meant to add to its performance. Willie Winkle, a famous Canadian skateboarder of the 1970s, worked with the company Sims to create the seven-ply maple boards that improved performance because of durability and responsiveness (to be explained later in this chapter) and that have become standard in the field today (Davis, 1999). Another board design innovation that added to performance was an upturn to the tail and nose of the board that created a slight concave shape. This nose and tail design creates leverage points that allow the skater to turn and flip the board more easily.

physics and skateboard design

Fundamental to skateboarding is momentum, as skateboarding is all about changing the position and speed of the board. Momentum is measured by the mass of an object and its velocity (speed and direction). It is determined by the mass of the skateboarder and equipment. Other forces affect how quickly the skateboarder loses or gains momentum, for example, air resistance (determined by the shape, size, and positioning of the skater's body) or the angle and texture of the surface one is riding.

The components of a skateboard are created with the concept of momentum in mind. For example, the wheels provide both traction and impact the speed of the board. The consistency of the wheel's material is crucial. According to physicist Paul Doherty, the wheel needs resiliency, which is the ability to bounce back to a circular shape upon contact with other materials such as pavement. Resiliency can be determined by the wheel's level of hardness. If the wheel is too soft and doesn't return to its circular shape quickly, it loses momentum and slows down the board (think of riding on a deflated tire). On the other hand, if the wheel is too hard, the pavement could warp, also causing a loss of momentum. Thus, a wheel that allows resiliency is fast and offers a smooth ride. Polyurethane is the material used in skateboard wheels because it provides resiliency and traction (Wanner, n.d.). Skateboarders can to some degree choose the hardness of their wheels depending on the type of ride they want. The hardness of a wheel is measured by testing the substance's resistance to penetration. A durometer measures the hardness of a wheel, which is then rated on a scale from 1 to 100, with 100 being the hardest. Skateboard wheels typically range from 70 to 101 in hardness. While softer wheels have a better grip, they wear out sooner and also develop flat spots.

The diameter of the wheel is measured in millimeters, most commonly in the range of 52 to 65 millimeters. Larger wheels roll faster and thus are most often used in vert skating, whereas smaller wheels are typically used for street skating, where technical tricks are key. Larger wheels handle bumps better because the angle of the force created from a pebble or crack is directed upward, causing a rough ride; with smaller wheels, the same force is directed backward, causing the board to stop. Yet larger wheels tend to be less resilient because the constant compressing and springing of the polyurethane takes energy, which slows the wheel down. To compensate, large wheels are usually wider, which increases their resiliency. That is why downhill boards, which are built for high levels of speed, have larger and wider wheels than street skateboards do (Skyler, 2007).

Additionally, momentum is aided by ball bearings that allow the wheel to spin without excessive friction. It wasn't until the mid-1970s that skateboard wheels came with precision-sealed bearings; before then, the bearings were not sealed, and skateboarders had to place them into the wheel manually.

Paul Schmitt has been making boards since he was 14 years old. He turned that passion into his business and has made over 13 million decks in his 30-year career. During his career as a skateboard manufacturer, he has produced decks for professional skaters such as Bob Burnquist, Ryan Sheckler, Paul Rodriguez, Jr., and Danny Way. His experience as a manufacturer and skater provides insight into factors that enhance board performance (personal interview with Schmitt, August 12, 2011). One of the key issues related to a traditional board used for tricks is to increase strength and keep weight low; enhancing the board's concave shape has done just this. In the late 1980s, Schmitt experimented with modifying the traditional triangulated concave shape. He modified the concave to be parallel and more balanced with both the nose and tail upturned. This structural refinement, in turn, affected the types of tricks one could perform. Prior to that, the nose was three to four inches long and could not be used for leverage. Afterward, skateboarders were able to perform tricks like the noseslide, nosegrind, nollie, and krooked grind.

Decks are also made with different degrees of flexibility. Longboards that are made for cruising have the most flexibility, as the rider generates momentum from pumping the board as opposed to relying solely on pushing one's foot against the ground to maintain or increase momentum. More flexibility in the board translates to a slower ride, as the flexible deck creates inefficient energy transfer, which reduces speed. Therefore, longboards made for downhill speed are less flexible. Regular skateboards also tend to be less flexible so that energy can be efficiently transferred to increase momentum. Boards made for the MegaRamp are thicker and stiffer so that they can handle higher speeds and higher G-forces, or the weight per unit of mass. Stability and strength are crucial for ramp riding. Therefore, decks used by MegaRamp skaters are about two inches longer in the wheelbase than a regular board and can include carbon fibers and Kevlar (personal interview with Schmitt, August 12, 2011).

Energy flow is another factor in deck design. Schmitt states that wood fiber configuration is one influence on energy flow and transfer. Most boards are made with seven-ply hard maple veneer. The wood fibers either follow the length of the board longitudinally or perpendicularly. In the 1970s, longitudinal fibers made up about 60 percent of a board; currently, that percentage is 80 percent, allowing for energy to be more effectively directed in the path of the board (personal interview with Schmitt, August 12, 2011).

physics of tricks

One of the main points of physics is explaining how matter moves through space. Physics can help explain how skateboarders are able to perform tricks, and it can also explain the possibilities and limits of skateboarding.

The ollie is a fundamental trick for street and vert skateboarding, as it allows a skateboarder to "jump" while maintaining control of the skateboard with his or her feet. To get maximum height, the skateboarder must bend his or her knees and then push hard off the ground quickly with the rear foot while the front foot is used primarily for control, not power. For the ollie, the initial stance is to have the rear foot on the tail of the board and the front foot slightly behind the front set of wheels, which can be easily identified by the location of the bolts on the board. The basic motion is to lower the body (and thus center of gravity) and then drive the rear foot down, pushing the tail of the board toward the ground while quickly extending the body by throwing the arms upward. Even though the skateboarder is powering the jump from the rear leg, he or she needs to use the front foot to direct the board. As the board pops, the front foot is dragged upward along the board toward the nose, which levels the board so that it is parallel with the ground.

When the tail hits the ground, it causes an opposite reaction, lifting the board off the ground. The momentum causes the board to rotate around the back axle, which lifts the nose of the board. The skater must lift the rear leg to allow the board to rise and use the front foot to stop the board from rotating around the back axle. This is done by sliding the front foot toward the nose of the board while maintaining contact. If the skater gets the timing right, it looks as if the board magically rises with the skater's feet (Tesler, 2007).

Another standard trick is a frontside 180. It is the trick that occurs in air where a skater turns around 180 degrees. This can occur when the skater is on a vert ramp. As the skater reaches the top of the ramp, he or she launches into the air, turns around in mid-air, and come back down to the ramp. Physicists would explain this movement through concepts of angular momentum and its conservation. The skater turns the board 180 degrees in mid-air by creating more inertia in the upper body so that the lower body (and board) need to turn faster. According to Tesler and Doherty (n.d), when the maneuver is performed correctly, the rotation of ones legs is countered by the rotation or ones outspread arms. the "large rotation of your legs" is "cancelled by a small rotation of your outspread arms":

> Since the two rotations cancel, angular momentum stays constant at zero, and the law of conservation of angular momentum is satisfied. Upon landing, a skater can use the friction between his or her feet and the skateboard to twist the upper body back into alignment. (Tesler & Doherty, n.d.)

Most skaters gain momentum by pushing off the ground with one foot as the other foot stays planted on the board. However, skaters in pools, bowls, and half pipes don't rely solely on this standard method; instead they pump the board. The pumping motion is like a piston. When the skater is in the flatter area in the pool, bowl, or half pipe, he or she bends down; then when the skater transitions to the steeper area, he or she stands up. Speed is crucial for gaining altitude, which allows skaters to pull off more impressive tricks in pools, bowls, and half pipes, such as Tony

Hawk's 900. This pumping motion enables the skater to raise his or her center of mass at the beginning of an arc. The centripetal force at this moment makes it harder to raise the body, making the skater work harder, which creates more energy and ultimately increases the speed of the board (Tesler & Doherty, n.d.).

the megaramp

A MegaRamp is a skateboard jump of enormous proportions; it is nine stories tall and over 100 yards long. Most skateboarding big air competitions use the MegaRamp. The skaters actually take an elevator to get to the top. It is composed of two main parts: the initial ramp and jump, which lead to a 70-foot gap and end with a 27-foot vertical ramp (called a quarter pipe). The MegaRamp is expensive to build and typically requires a lot of time and resources to set up. Because of the expense and space requirements, there are few permanent MegaRamps, making it difficult for most skaters to have a chance to practice on one. A few skaters who are known for this event are Danny Way (who jumped the Great Wall of China with this item in 2005), Bob Burnquist, Jake Brown, and Lyn-Z Adams Hawkins Pastrana. Skateboarders have been

MegaRamp used for the X Games. (AP Photo/Kevork Djansezian)

clocked going 44 miles per hour at the bottom of the ramp. It's the height of the ramp that allows the skater to gain such speed. And it's done by converting potential energy into kinetic energy. At the top of the ramp, the skater has potential energy; once he or she drops in and starts rolling, that potential energy gets converted to kinetic energy.

But is there a limit to how fast a skater can go? Will building bigger jumps translate into skateboarders going faster and higher? Physicist Paul Doherty suggests two main physical limitations. First is the concept of terminal velocity, or simply put the limit to an object's acceleration. Air resistance ultimately slows a falling object, and air resistance increases with speed, so at some point a falling object reaches a maximum speed. Based on the terminal velocity of sky divers, Doherty states that even ramps over 1,000 feet high won't increase a skater's terminal velocity, which would be about 120 miles per hour (in Tesler, 2007). Another factor that limits ramp design is the G-forces created. G-forces refer to acceleration that exceeds the force of gravity. The human body can handle only so much force; at about five times the amount of gravity, people tend to black out. At the base of the current MegaRamp, skaters feel about 2.5 G-forces. With a taller ramp and higher speeds, the G-forces would increase. To make the experience tolerable, the ramp structure would have to change to have more gradual curves (Tesler, 2007).

media technology

Although media technology doesn't directly impact physical negotiation of the urban landscape, it is crucial in the social landscape. Videos are central to skateboarding in several ways. First, videos created by corporations have set a standard for skills and set a tone of what is "authentic" to skateboarding culture (Dinces, 2011). The Powell Peralta videos of the Bones Brigade team during the 1980s demonstrated how powerful this medium could be. Not only did the videos sell better than anticipated, they became the standard way of advertising in the industry. Virtually all major skate corporations put out videos that highlight their sponsored skaters (and the equipment the skaters are using).

In addition to the act of skateboarding, one main way skaters socialize is to watch skate videos together, and favorite videos can be watched hundreds of times (Beal & Wilson, 2004; Dinces, 2011). In this way, videos are educational and inspirational, for they introduce skaters to the culture and showcase top talent as well as cutting-edge tricks.

Dave Carulli, right, rolls on a skateboard while taking video of Justin Funk as he
does tricks along a sidewalk in downtown Pittsburgh, November 11, 2010.
The two make videos and post them on the Internet. They try to sell them as well.
(AP Photo/Keith Srakocic)

During the early and mid-1990s, video technology became reasonably
priced and compact enough that skaters could put cameras in their back-
packs and document their own skateboarding. Skateboard shops often
have their own video production teams, film local talent, and play the
resultant videos in their stores. This plays off the culture of watching

videos together and draws in a local customer base. Currently, video technology is mobile and less expensive as it went from using VHS tape to hard drives to store images. It is rare to find a crew skating that doesn't include someone filming. A common dynamic is to film skaters doing tough tricks, and if a friend makes the trick there is cheering, immediately followed by watching a replay of it from the hard drive—and cheering again.

In addition to the pleasure of watching the videos, skaters use them as a means of attaining visual feedback to improve their skating techniques. Additionally, videos are "proof" that one either attempted or made a particular trick. Part of skateboard culture is highlighting the desire to improve through risktaking. Thus, spectacular falls and crashes are standard fare in videos (Walk, 2006). Videos are seen as more legitimate means of documenting skill than photos because still shots don't substantiate the success of the trick: a nice mid-air shot does not mean the skater landed the trick. Finally, sharing the video clip is the key way to solidify and expand one's reputation. Even among professionals, videos are the most important means of establishing one's legitimacy among peers and the industry. One classic video can make a skater's reputation for life. For example, Mark Gonzales's skating in Blind's *Video Days* (1991) still carries weight among seasoned skaters. Video exposure is so important that the relationship between professional skaters and videographers is often close based on clear communication and respect. Practically all skate videographers were skateboarders, and professional skaters often choose their own photographer/videographer based on trust developed over time (personal interview with Mike Rafter, August 15, 2011).

There is no doubt that technological advances have impacted the style, scale, and social worlds of skateboarders. A working knowledge of physics and a video camera to document one's attempts at an ollie or a frontside 180 can be beneficial and fun. Ultimately, being able to perform any trick comes through trial and error. Skateboarders develop a feel or an intuitive sense about their bodies and boards only through actual practice. Even Paul Schmitt, the renowned deck manufacturer, states that the ultimate test of a good deck is not a mechanical analysis but simply to ride the board.

technologies of discipline

While all the physical technologies described previously are crucial to navigating the built environment, just as important is how the social environment "disciplines" or regulates these physical spaces. This concept of discipline is drawn from the work of Michael Foucault and refers to the social processes that direct our bodies to move and act in particular ways. In other words, one's use of equipment, places, and skate obstacles is impacted by the amount and type of social constraints faced, such as legal status and gender norms.

deterrents

The most obvious disciplining technique is the legal status of skateboarding. In many public places, skateboarding is illegal and police are able to ticket offenders (Chiu, 2009; Woolley, Hazelwood, & Simkins, 2011). Notwithstanding, legal status has rarely stopped people from skateboarding in public places. As noted previously, the city landscape of stairs, handrails, benches, planters, and parking blocks is a virtual playground that invites people to sidestep the law and skate. Skateboarding on these elements does cause some damage. In response, some businesses have created antiskate devices. These are usually metal knobs or brackets that one can connect to skateable architecture to disrupt the flow and trip up skaters. Because the original stoppers were not aesthetically pleasing, companies have developed custom designs. For example, in San Francisco's Fisherman's Wharf area, skate stoppers are in the shape of starfish, turtles, and octopi. Not surprisingly, skaters have found ways to remove these items and share that information widely on social media such as YouTube. Or some engage in covert activities, for example, the Skatespot Liberation Front detaches antiskate devices and creatively alters "No Skateboarding" signs by putting a *G* in place of the *N* to form "Go Skateboarding" signs (Vivoni, 2009).

Over the past 60 years, groups of teenagers have often been framed as potential troublemakers, and thus increased regulation is deemed necessary (Chiu, 2009; Valentine, 1996; Willard, 1998). The desire to oversee teenagers' behavior may be one of the reasons publicly funded skate parks have become popular (Howell, 2008). The official sanctioning of particular parks creates a clear mandate from municipal officials to funnel and manage skateboarders' activities. Public skate parks have rules and regulations, and often are supervised by adults. Additionally, they tend to be placed outside of city centers, relegating skateboarders to the margins. The setup of parks tends to provide more surveillance and regulation. A 19-year-old skater commented: "It is like a cage. Every skate park is like a cage. You have to wear a helmet. It's kind of like a forced environment" (in Chiu, 2009, 38).

Interestingly, although adult supervision may go against the ethos of independence, risktaking, and creativity of skateboarding, it also may open opportunities for those who have historically been marginalized. Often girls and the youngest participants don't have strong social networks that support skateboarding. It has been found that formal skate parks with adult supervision are more inclusive (Dumas & Laforest, 2009; Reinhart & Grenfell, 2002).

When it comes to using public space, the influence of social networks can greatly affect who and how different skate spots are used. Social science research has shown that male networks have been employed to largely keep females from skating the most coveted spots and from being the center of media attention (Atencio, Beal, & Wilson, 2009; Pomerantz, Currie, & Kelly 2004; Porter, 2003; Rinehart, 2005). Many females interviewed by social scientists would talk about how boys often harassed them if they were in a public skateboard space. One informant, Michelle, for instance, noted that "I am the only girl that ever skates at my park. There aren't a lot of girl skaters. I mean wherever you go you are usually fighting (with the men) for a spot" (in Atencio et al., 2009, 12). This battle over space was echoed by another teenaged skater, Carly, who noted that the men made skateboarding spaces uncomfortable for the women by challenging their knowledge of the sport and treating females "like dogs" (in Atencio et al., 2009, 13). A female skater from Canada asserted, "Every time I venture out to skate, either alone or with friends, I am in some way harassed, threatened or opposition to my skating is voiced in some manner" (in Pomerantz et al., 2004, 550).

These types of exclusionary practices have encouraged females to create skate spaces of their own. At the forefront of that movement was Patty Segovia-Krause, who began the All Girl Skate Jam in 1996. Many others have picked up on the idea and replicated the premise, but in different venues like Girl Riders Organization (GRO) and Skirtboarders (see chapter 2, "Origins and Development"). These have been popular because they are a means to create social networks that encourage and support female skaters. One female skater explained the value of female-designated skateboard spaces in this way:

It (female only spaces) is definitely in a positive way. I am pretty sure that it is one of the only skate competitions where girls actually get prizes. Like the amateurs will get snowboards, skateboards, surfboards and the pros will get money. It's awesome. Definitely for the better, like I have met a lot of girls. If I see a girl skating, I'll be like "Oh my gosh." I will write down all the websites for her and like let her know she isn't the only girl skate boarding 'cause you never see any girls skateboarding and you start to think you are the only one. And I will tell them about all the websites and say, "You're not the only one out there, swear to God!" and try to get them out. It is definitely a good thing. Definitely a good feel to it. (Atencio et al., 2009, 14)

Science and technology help explain how skateboarders navigate their environments. But this navigation is always done within a social context. Societal power and cultural norms affect one's access to skate spots as well as one's access to a social network of skaters. Both types of access provide opportunities that are crucial in developing skills.

6.   future trends

the future trends of skateboarding will be driven by how participants, professional skateboarders, and industry members address internal tensions and how businesses develop and expand the sport as well as related products. The key tension is between the desire to develop a consumer base and the desire to maintain skateboarding's alternative and cool image (Chivers Yochim, 2010). This tension gets played out in several ways and, fundamentally, points to which stakeholders have the most power to affect the direction of skateboarding.

tensions within professional skateboarding

One of the key tensions within professional skateboarding is who controls and who benefits from it. There are two levels of struggle. One is at the organizational level, where there have been ongoing disputes over which group is the "official" governing body of skateboarding. World Cup Skateboarding (WCS) has positioned itself to do this but continues to be challenged by others. WCS has aligned its structure according to International Olympic Committee standards so that it could potentially act as the governing body that would determine who would qualify for the Olympics if skateboarding were ever to be included. The Maloof Money Cup, which has the largest purse, has recently disassociated from WCS. And the Street League, which was organized by Rob Dyrdek, is in competition with both the WCS and Maloof Money Cup because of the no competition clause that athletes must sign. In other words, if one competes for Street League, he or she cannot enter any other major contests. Additionally, the Street League is the only organization that offers profit sharing to its skaters. This leads to the second level of struggle: skater and management disputes. Male professional skateboarders have at times threatened to boycott events if salaries weren't raised, and women have organized, for example, through the Action Sports Alliance, to work for equity in salary and on-air exposure with their male peers. Additionally, professional status is determined primarily by an athlete's sponsor. For example, different companies sponsor both amateur and professional teams. They make judgments about a skater's status based not only on the athlete's skill, but also based on the athlete's persona and how it represents the company. In other words, professional status is not based on a purely meritocratic system. It is impacted largely by what type of brand the company wants to present.

Even though the struggle of who controls skateboarding will continue, there is common ground among the corporate stakeholders: they want skateboarding to be seen as a legitimate sport. Further institutionalization and globalization will expand, as is evidenced by such organizations as the International Association of Skateboarding Companies and its efforts to create the international Go Skate Day and establish an international hall of fame. Globalization of competitions such as the X Games and the Maloof Money Cup as well as camps such as Woodward will proliferate. Corporations will continue to help subsidize skate parks; Rob Dyrdek and Tony Hawk have their own foundations, which are currently doing this. The Maloofs are also donating skate parks they build for their competitions to the cities that host them. Parks are essential to providing opportunities for people to learn to skate. Thus, establishing skate parks is supporting the growth of the sport.

Another form of ongoing institutionalization will happen in the cultural realm. Skateboarding-themed forms of art will continue to be promoted by the industry. Some examples include corporations such as RVCA and Nike sponsoring art; RVCA publishes *ANP Quarterly*, and Nike has sponsored several art exhibits, including the *Beautiful Losers*. Others such as Vans and Quiksilver have been underwriting documentary films. Vans partially funded *Dogtown and Z-Boys*, while Quiksilver partially funded *Rising Son*. A group of prominent skateboarders and artists—including Craig Stecyk, Stacy Peralta, Ed Templeton, and Grant Brittain—recently started the Academy of Skateboard Film Makers, Arts and Sciences, which hosts an international skateboard film festival. These artistic expressions help establish a history and folklore which, in turn, infuses skateboarding into our broader culture.

trends to establish a wider consumer base

This artistic and cultural infusion also serves as a means to sell skateboarding products. Essentially, selling skateboarding products incorporates selling particular storylines or value sets. Corporations develop and use different product storylines to attract different groups of consumers. One of the major continuing trends is to infuse skateboarding into a complete lifestyle. This means that skateboarding becomes more than a pastime; instead, it is a way of life or a symbol of one's values and identity. Skateboard corporations have been working on this premise for a while.

One of the more common forms of fostering a lifestyle around skateboarding has been to create a festival environment. With most competitions, a variety of entertainment, especially music, art, and film, are featured along with skateboarding. Another example of integrating entertainment and skateboarding can be found in video games. These games are not only fun to play, but they serve to socialize consumers about the culture of skateboarding by introducing them to professional skaters (avatars), revered locations such as the Burnside Bridge, and products that are strategically placed throughout the games. Recently, Mountain Dew built a skate park in Auckland, New Zealand, that was designed to look like an old-fashioned pinball machine ("Pinball Skatepark," 2011).

The marketing of skateboarding has historically been geared toward teenage and young adult males (Browne, 2004; Chivers Yochim, 2010). Because of the desire to increase revenues, the industry will continue to develop niche or specialized markets. As mentioned in chapter 2 on origins and development, a variety of skateboarding styles is being embraced such as longboarding and pool riding. Additionally, diverse groups of people are claiming their own place within skateboarding. For example, there are organizations for older people, for girls, for moms, for people with disabilities, and for different religious affiliations. As noted in chapter 3 on venues for creativity, different ethnic groups are claiming their space and voice within skateboarding through art exhibitions. This trend toward diversification of the market will continue, but nonetheless there will still be conversation related to which types of skateboarding (and skateboarders) are more "authentic" or "core," which translates into which groups get the most media coverage, competitive opportunities, and rewards. Thus, a diverse consumer base does not equate to equitable treatment among various consumer groups.

Perhaps an example of the ultimate integration of skateboarding into daily life may be the PAS skateboarding house, which was envisioned by Pierre-Andre Senizergues (PAS), the owner of Etnie's skateboarding brands and former professional skateboarder. The architect is Francois Perrin, and a model of part of the house was exhibited at a Paris cultural and community center, La Faite Lyrique. The actual house will be built in Malibu, California. The basic structure is a tube, which creates easily skateable circular surfaces. Even the appliances will have rounded edges to enable their skateability. The furniture will also be constructed with recycled skateboard decks and wheels from a retailer that specializes in this (Fisher, 2011).

sustainability

Skateboarders and the industry are starting to address their environmental impact. Many longboarders who use skateboarding primarily as a means of transportation are arguing that it is eco-friendly and should be supported by local governments (Dehaas, 2010). Specific companies such as Comet Skateboards are advertising their products as being based on green practices, including materials being sustainably harvested and biodegradable composites being used instead of petroleum-based products (Netravali, 2008). Professional athletes have organized to promote community support and education programs around sustainability. One example is the Action Sports Environmental Coalition. Sustainability is a broader social issue than skateboarding; nonetheless, skateboarding's DIY and democratic ethos will play a part in the industry's support of environmentalism.

public sector

While private industry is promoting skateboarding brands and products, the public sector such as local governments are also using skateboarding as a means to reach youth. Their goal is not to sell products, but to provide safe places to skate and other resources. In the United States and Canada, public skate parks have generally been supported as a form of safety and control in hopes of keeping youth off the streets and out of trouble (Dumas & Laforest, 2009; Howell, 2008; Willard, 1998). The idea of using skateboarding as part of overall youth development has been taken several steps further in Merida, Spain. A youth center called Factoria Joven opened in March 2011. It has been designed so that a skate plaza connects all the buildings, with most surfaces skateable. The architect called it an "open factory of ideas, urban art, and sport" (Verghese, n.d., para 1). The facility not only caters to youth activities like skateboarding, rock climbing, graffiti, computer and internet use, parkour, an activity in which the built environment is traversed without specialized equipment, and the performing arts, but it is also a resource and counseling center. The design of the building is intentionally engaging for young people so that they will seek out assistance and stay out of trouble (Oksana, 2011).

When the public sector becomes involved, a more paternalistic emphasis is present, as safety becomes the primary concern. For some skaters, this may be the antithesis of the independent, DIY ethos frequently attributed to the sport. This tension between public sanction and self-governance is continually illustrated by the legal status of the sport. Even though much of the public sector has embraced skateboarding as a positive activity for youth, it has done so by separating skateboarding from the ebb and flow of city life by creating segregated and often adult-supervised spaces. Skateboarding in most public spaces is still illegal. This prohibition is being extended to downhill longboarders who use public streets. The frustration of this apparent double standard is expressed by one Los Angeles longboarder: "No one seems to mind it when street bikes or mountain bikes come down a hill at 50 mph. It takes them up to 50 feet to stop. I can stop in 10 feet from the same speed" (in Roper, 2011, para 7). Debates over the use of public space will continue.

With skateboarding capturing the mainstream imagination, many entities have used its appeal. Unrelated corporations, such as those in the fast-food industry, use skateboarding to sell products to a youth audience. The sport is used by the public sector to reach a youth audience with the intent of providing safety or education. It is also used by the media, such as ESPN and video game companies, to create entertainment products. And skateboarders use the sport to socialize and be physically active. Skateboarding, like all social activities, changes. With the multitude of interests involved, its meaning and forms will continue to be debated and altered, creating shifts, fractures, and expansion in the significance and shape of skateboarding.

resource guide

this guide is constructed to help those who are doing further research on skateboarding to easily identify resources. The past 15 years have seen a proliferation of academic research on skateboarding and other extreme, action, or alternative sports. Research that has focused on skateboarding is provided in the following sections. Although there is some overlap with the book's bibliography, many entries are exclusive to this resource guide. Also included are a number of books, magazines, films, and websites dedicated to skateboarding.

academic sources: books

Booth, D., & Thorpe, H. (Eds.) (2007). *Berkshire Encyclopedia of Extreme Sport*. Great Barrington, MA: Berkshire Publishing.

Borden, I. (2001). *Skateboarding, Space and the City: Architecture and the Body*. Oxford: Berg Publishers.

Chivers Yochim, E. (2010). *Skate Life: Re-Imagining White Masculinity*. Ann Arbor: University of Michigan Press.

Laurent, J. (2012). *Le Skateboard: Analyse Sociologique d'une Practique Physique Urbaine: This Is Street Skateboarding*. Paris: L'Harmattan.

Rinehart, R., & Sydnor, S. (Eds.). (2003). *To the Extreme: Alternative Sports, Inside and Out*. Albany: State University of New York (SUNY) Press.

Wheaton, B. (Ed.). (2004). *Understanding Lifestyle Sports: Consumption, Identity, and Difference*. London: Routledge Press.

Wheaton, B. (forthcoming). *Lifestyle Sport: The Cultural Politics of Alternative Sports*. London: Routledge Press.

academic sources: journal articles and book chapters

Atencio, M., & Beal, B. (2011) "Beautiful Losers": The symbolic exhibition and legitimization of outsider masculinity. *Sport and Society, 14*, 1–16.

Atencio, M., Beal, B., & Wilson, C. (2009). Distinction of risk: Urban skateboarding, street habitus, and the construction of hierarchical gender relations. *Qualitative Research in Sport and Exercise, 1*, 3–20.

Beal, B. (1995). Disqualifying the official: An exploration of social resistance in the subculture of skateboarding. *Sociology of Sport Journal, 12*, 252–267.

Beal, B. (1996). Alternative masculinity and its effects on gender relations in the subculture of skateboarding. *Journal of Sport Behavior, 19*, 204–220.

Beal, B., & Weidman, L. (2003). Authenticity in the skateboarding world. In R. Rinehart & S. Sydnor (Eds.), *To the Extreme: Alternative Sports, Inside and Out* (pp. 337–352). Albany: SUNY Press.

Beal, B., & Wilson, C. (2004). "Chicks dig scars": Commercialisation and the transformations of skate boarders' identities. In B. Wheaton (Ed.), *Understanding Lifestyle Sports: Consumption, Identity and Difference* (pp. 31–54). London: Routledge.

Bennett, Greg, and Lachowetz, Tony (2004). Marketing to lifestyles: Action sports and Generation Y. *Sport Marketing Quarterly*, 13, 239–243.

Bradley, G. (2010). Skate parks as context for adolescent development. *Journal of Adolescent Research, 25*, 288–323.

Brayton, Sean (2005). "Black-lash": Revisiting the "White Negro" through skateboarding. *Sociology of Sport Journal, 22*, 356–372.

Chiu, Chihsin (2009). Contestation and conformity: Street and park skating in New York City public space. *Space and Culture, 12*, 25–42.

Davidson, J. (1985). Sport and modern technology: The rise of skateboarding, 1963–1978. *Journal of Popular Culture, 18*, 145–157.

Dumas, A., & Laforest, S. (2009). Skateparks as health resource: Are they as dangerous as they look? *Leisure studies, 28*, 19–34.

Howell, O. (2005). The "creative class" and the gentrifying city: Skateboarding in Philadelphia's Love Park. *Journal of Architectural Education, 59*(2), 32–42.

Howell, O. (2008). Skatepark as neoliberal playground: Urban governance, recreation space, and cultivation of personal responsibility. *Space and Culture, 11*, 475–496.

Howell, Ocean. Extreme market research: Tales from the underbelly of skater-cool. *Topic Magazine*, 4. Retrieved from http:/ http://www.webdelsol.com/Topic/articles/04/howell.html.

Irvine, S., & Taysom, S. (1998). Skateboarding: Disrupting the city. *Social Alternatives, 17*, 23–26.

Karsten, L., and Pel, E. (2000). Skateboarders exploring public space: Ollies, obstacles and conflicts. *Journal of Housing and the Built Environment*, 15, 327–340.

Kelly, D., Pomerantz, S., & Currie, D. (2005). Skater girlhood and emphasized femininity: "You can't land an ollie properly in heels." *Gender and Education, 17*(3), 129–148.

Lombard, K. J. (2010). Skate and create/skate and destroy: The commercial and governmental incorporation of skateboarding. *Continuum: Journal of Media & Cultural Studies, 24*, 475–488.

Nemeth, J. (2006). Conflict, exclusion, relocation: Skateboarding and public space. *Journal of Urban Design, 11*(3), 297–318.

Nolan, N. (2003). The ins and outs of skateboarding and transgression in public space in Newcastle, Australia. *Australian Geographer, 34*(3), 311–327.

Porter, N. (2003). Female skateboarders and their negotiation of space and identity. *Journal for Arts, Sciences, and Technology, 1*, 75–80.

Rinehart, Robert (2000). Emerging Arriving Sport: Alternatives to Formal Sport. In J. Coakley and E. Dunning (Eds.), *Handbook of Sport Studies* (pp. 504–519). London: Sage.

Rinehart, Robert (2005). "Babes" & boards: Opportunities in new millennium sport? *Journal of Sport and Social Issues, 29*, 232–255.

Seifert, T. & Henderson, C. (2010). Intrinsic motivation and flow in skateboarding: An ethnographic study. *Journal of Happiness Studies, 11*, 277–292.

Smith, M., and Beal, B. (2007). "So you can see how the other half lives": MTV "Cribs' " use of "the other" in framing successful athletic masculinities. *Journal of Sport and Social Issues*, 31, 103–127.

Stratford, E. (2002). On the edge: A tale of skaters and urban governance. *Social and Cultural Geography*, *3*(2), 193–206.

Taylor, M., & Khan, U. (2011). Skate-park builds, teenaphobia and the adolescent need for hang-out spaces: The social utility and functionality of urban skate parks. *Journal of Urban Design, 16*, 489–510.

Thorpe, H. (2006). Beyond "decorative sociology": Contextualizing female surf, skate, and snow boarding. *Sociology of Sport Journal, 23*, 205–228.

Thorpe, H., & Wheaton, B. (2011). The Olympic movement, action sports and the search for Generation Y. In J. Sugden & A. Tomlinson (Eds.), *Watching the Olympics: Politics, Power and Representation* (pp. 182–200). London: Routledge.

Vivoni, F. (2009). Sports of spatial desires: Skateparks, skateplazas and urban politics. *Journal of Sport and Social Issues, 33*, 130–149.

Weller, S. (2006). Skateboarding alone? Making social capital discourse relevant to teenagers lives. *Journal of Youth Studies, 9*, 557–574.

Wheaton, Belinda. (2005). Selling out? The commercialization and globalization of lifestyle sport. In L. Allison (Ed.), *The Global Politics of Sport: The Role of Global Institutions in Sport* (pp. 140–185). London: Routledge.

Wheaton, B. (2010). Introducing the consumption and representation of lifestyle sports. *Sport in Society, 13*, 1057–1081.

Wheaton, B., & Beal, B. (2003). "Keeping it real": Subcultural media and the discourses of authenticity in alternative sport. *International Review for the Sociology of Sport, 38*, 155–176.

Willard, M. N. (1998). Séance, tricknowlogy, skateboarding, and the space of youth. In J. Austin & M. N. Willard (Eds.), *Generations of Youth: Youth Cultures and History in Twentieth-Century America* (pp. 327–346). New York: New York University Press.

Woolley, H., & Johns, R. (2001). Skateboarding: The city as a playground. *Journal of Urban Design, 6*, 211–230.

Woolley, H., Hazelwood, T., & Simkins, I. (2011). Don't skate here: The exclusion of skateboarders from urban civic spaces in three northern cities in England. *Journal of Urban Design, 16*, 471–487.

Young, Alana, & Dalliare, Christine (2008). Beware*#!Sk8 at your own risk: The discourses of young female skateboarders. In M. Atkinson & K. Young (Eds.), *Tribal play: Subcultural journeys through sport* (pp. 235–254). Bingley UK: Emerald Group Publishing.

popular books: general overview of skateboarding

Brooke, Michael (1999). *The Concrete Wave: The History of Sskateboarding*. Toronto: Warwick Publishing.

Browne, Don (2004). *Amped: How Big Air, Big Dollars and a New Generation Took Sports to the Extreme*. New York: Bloomsbury.

Davis, James (2004). *Skateboarding Is Not a Crime: 50 Years of Street Culture*. Buffalo, NY: Firefly Books.

Mortimer, S. (2008). *Stalefish: Skateboard Culture from the Rejects Who Made It*. San Francisco: Chronicle Books.

Smith, J. (Ed). (2009). *Lives on Board*. Morrow Bay, CA: Morrow Skateboard Group.

Walsh, B., & Tison, M. (2006). *Pipe Fiends: A Visual Overdose of Montreal's Most Infamous Skate Spot*. Montreal: Mudscout Media.

Weyland, J. (2002). *The Answer Is Never: A Skateboarder's History of the World*. New York: Grove Press.

popular books: skate/art

Caron, T. (Ed). (2010). *Ed Templeton: Cemetery of Reason*. S.M.A.K. New York, NY: D.A.P. Distributed Art Publishers

Cliver, S. (2007). *Disposable: A History of Skateboard Art*. Berkeley, CA: Gingko Press

Cliver, S. (2009). *The Disposable Skateboard Bible*. Berkeley, CA: Gingko Press.

Corporan, A., Razzo, A., & Serra, I. (Eds.). (2010). *Full Bleed: New York City Skateboard Photography*. Brooklyn, NY: Vice Magazine and Powerhouse Books.

Howell, A. (2006). *Art, Skateboarding and Life*. Berkeley, CA: Gingko Press.

Phillips, J. (2007). *The Skateboard Art of Jim Phillips*. Atglen, PA: Schiffer Publishing Ltd.

Rose, Aaron, and Strike, Christian (Eds.). (2004). *Beautiful Losers: Contemporary Art and Street Culture*. New York: Iconoclast and Distributed Art Publishers, Inc.

Templeton, Ed. (2005). *Golden Age of Neglect*. Rome: Drago.

popular books: biography and autobiographies

Hawk, T. (2000). *Hawk: Occupation: Skateboarder*. Regan Books.

Hawk, T., & Hawk, P. (2010). *How Did I Get Here? The Ascent of an Unlikely CEO*. John Wiley and Sons.

Mullen, R. (2004). *Mutt: How to Skateboard and Not Kill Yourself*. Regan Books.

Templeton, Ed. (2008). *Deformer*. Damiani.

canadian and u.s. skateboard magazines:

Concrete Skateboarding, Concrete Wave, Expose, Focus, Huck, Juice, SBC Skateboard, Skateboarding, The Skateboard Mag, Slap, Thrasher, Transworld Skateboarding

skateboarding in film

Skateboarding in film has been used in several ways: as a means to capture a youth audience, as a means to document the culture, and as a means of promoting the activity. In many of the films, all three are happening but to different degrees. This list is not comprehensive but provides a representation of various skate films.

documentaries

Skateboard Kings (1978). Produced for the BBC television series called *The World Around Us*.

Explores the skateboarding scene in Los Angeles.

Dogtown and Z-Boys (2001). Directed by Stacy Peralta.

Examines the role that southern California and the Z-Boys had on the culture of skateboarding.

Stoked (2002). Directed by Helen Stickler.

Addresses the life of renowned 1980s skateboarder Mark Rogowski, who was sentenced to 31 years in federal prison for killing his girlfriend.

Rising Son: The Legend of Skateboarder Christian Hosoi (2006). Directed by Cesario Montano.

Explores the rise and fall of a legendary 1980s skater who gets hooked on crystal meth and gets arrested and jailed, but eventually cleans up, converts to Christianity, and is released from jail.

Bones Brigade: An Autobiography (2012). Directed by Stacy Peralta.

Explores the lives of the six skaters (Steve Caballero, Tommy Guerroro, Tony Hawk, Mike McGill, Lance Mountain, and Rodney Mullen) who starred in the famous video series of the 1980s.

films that focus on skateboarding

The Devil's Toy (1966). Directed by Claude Jutra.

A short film based in Montreal that depicts skaters as rebellious and fighting against police.

Freewheelin' (1976). Directed by Scott Dittrich.

This movie is a cross between a documentary and a drama. It features great skaters of that era such as Russ Howell, Mike Weed, Marty Grimes, and Stacy Peralta but has a minimal storyline.

Wassup Rockers (2005). Directed by Larry Clark.

Follows a group of male Hispanic teenage friends who skateboard, highlighting how they negotiate racial tensions in southern California.

Paranoid Park (2007). Directed by Gus Van Sant.

The film is set in Portland, Oregon, and uses Burnside Bridge skate park. The main plot is about a teenaged male skateboarder who is implicated in the murder of a security guard.

films that use skateboarding to address youth culture

Skater Dater (1965). Directed by Noel Black.

This is a short film that won best short at Cannes Film Festival in 1966. There is no dialogue, but the film does feature surf/skate music. It focuses on a young male skater who deals with peer pressure and tough choices.

Skateboard (1978). Directed by George Gage.

This film is about a man who owes lots of money to a bookie. He develops a skateboard team and enters them in a competition in hopes of winning so that he can pay his debts. The film stars Leif Garret and features the skating of Tony Alva and Ellen O'Neal.

Thrashin' (1986). Directed by David Winters.

Two rival skateboard gangs engage in conflict as they prepare for a contest. One skater, played by Josh Brolin, falls in love with a sister of a skater from the rival gang. The soundtrack features bands such as the Red Hot Chili Peppers and the Circle Jerks. Chrstian Hosoi, Lance Moutnatin, Eddie Reategui, Steve Olson, and Tony Alva are some of the top skaters used in the film.

Gleaming the Cube (1989). Directed by Graeme Clifford.

This film is about a teenaged white skater who is a slacker. But when his adopted Vietnamese brother is found dead, the skater (played by Christian Slater) decides he needs to solve the crime. This film features many top skateboarders, especially from the Bones Brigade, for the skating scenes.

Grind (2003). Directed by Casey La Scala.

A group of friends who just finished high school decide to go after their dreams of becoming professional skateboarders by taking a road trip to follow a professional skateboarder in hopes of getting noticed.

websites

| About.com | www.skateboard.about.com/ |
| Adaptive Action Sports | http://adacs.org/ |

The Action Sports Alliance	http://www.actionsportsalliance.com/
The Berrics	www.berrics.com
BNQT	www.BQNT.com
ESPN Action Sports	http://espn.go.com/action/
I Skate Therefore I Am	http://poolrider.blogspot.com

glossary

skateboard components

bushings.   Part of the trucks (axle mechanism) that allows for turning. It is a urethane doughnut-shaped device within the truck that allows for pivoting and thus turning.

deck.   The actual board on which one stands; is most often made of wood. Decks come in a variety of shapes and sizes depending on the style of ride the skateboarder desires (see chapter 5, navigating the built environment, for more information).

grip tape.   Sandpaper-like material that is fixed to the top of the deck to increase traction between the skateboard and the skater's feet, enabling the skater to hold on to, or "grip," the board, which allows for more control.

nose.   The front of the skateboard.

rail.   The edge of the skateboard; historically, the plastic strips attached to the board's underside.

tail.   The rear of the skateboard.

trucks.   The front and rear axle mechanism (including bushings) that connects the wheels to the deck and allows for turns.

wheels.   Usually made of polyurethane and connected to the trucks (axles). Wheels come in different diameters and hardness depending on the style of ride the skateboarder desires (see chapter 5, navigating the built environment, for more information).

wheelbase.   The distance between the front and back wheels, measured between the two sets of innermost truck holes. Shorter wheelbases allow for tighter turns and often are associated with street skateboarding, whereas long wheelbases have wider turns and generally are used for downhill speed.

skateboard tricks

For visuals of these tricks, see the video at the website http://theberrics .com/trickipedia.

180, 360, 720, 900.   These numbers refer to the degree of spin of either the board or the skateboarder. For example, a 360 occurs when the board is spun around one full rotation.

air.   Riding with all four wheels off the ground; frequently achieved by performing an ollie or by riding vertical (ramps) terrain.

backside.   When a trick or turn is executed with the skater's back facing the ramp or obstacle.

boning.   A tweak to a trick accomplished by straightening one or both legs while in mid-air.

caballerial.   A 360-degree turn performed on a ramp while riding fakie (backward), named after skater Steve Caballero.

carve.   To skate in a long curving arc similar to an *S* shape. Frequently done by longboarders while going downhill.

coping.   Rounded section of pipe that is attached to smooth out the edges (or lips) of the half pipe or ramps allowing for smoother grinds.

drop in.   Motion used when starting a run into a vert ramp or pool.

fakie.   When a skater is rolling backward—the skater is standing in his or her normal stance, but the board is moving backward. This is different from a switch stance (see later in this glossary).

frontside.   When a trick or turn is executed with the front of the skater's body facing the ramp or obstacle.

goofyfoot.   Riding with the right foot forward, the opposite of regular foot.

grab.   Touching the board during a trick.

  indy grab.   Skater leans forward, bending from the waist, and grabs the board between his or her feet.

method grab. Skater grabs the heelside of the board with his or her leading hand.

nose grab. Skater grabs the nose of the board.

grind. Sliding along on a curb, railing, or other surface, usually involving scraping one or both axles (trucks).

crooked grind. Grinding on only the front truck while sliding.

50-50 grind. Grinding on both trucks equally.

nosegrind. grinding on only the front truck.

5-0 grind. Grinding on only the back truck.

smith grind. a rear truck grind, with the nose pointed below and slightly away from the obstacle.

heelflip. A kickflip in which the skater uses the front heel to flip the board in the opposite direction.

japan air. The skater grabs the toeside edge of the deck behind the front trucks with his or her front hand then drops his or her knees, bending the body so that the board is now behind the skater's body.

kickflip. A variation on the ollie in which the skater ollies and spins the board 360 degrees before landing back on it.

mctwist. A 540-degree turn performed on a ramp, named after Mike McGill.

manual. While riding, one lifts the front of the board so that only the back wheels are touching the ground.

mongo-foot. A style of pushing where the back foot is kept on the board and pushing is done with the front foot.

nollie. An ollie performed by tapping the nose of the board instead of the tail.

nose manual. While riding, one lifts the back of the board so that only the front wheels are touching the ground.

noseslide. Sliding the underside of the nose end of a board on a ledge or lip.

ollie. Propelling the board in the air by tapping the tail of the board on the ground; the basis of most skating tricks.

railslide. A trick in which the skater slides the underside of the deck along an object, such as a curb or handrail.

regular foot. Riding with the left foot forward, the opposite of goofyfoot.

rock n roll. A lip tick. The skater rides up to the edge of the ramp with the front trucks over the coping. If the rider drops back in, he or she is in fakie position, and the trick is called rock to fakie. If the skater pivots, turns the board 180 degrees, and rolls back down with the front foot forward, to is referred to as rock n roll.

shifty. A maneuver to add flare to tricks. It involves rotating the board in mid-air and returning to normal position without using one's hands. Instead, the skater uses hip rotation and his or her feet to control the board.

shove-it. A trick performed by spinning the board 180 degrees beneath the feet while traveling forward.

sliding. A technique used by downhill longboarders to stop momentum. Similar to a ski stop, it involves quickly spinning the board perpendicular to the initial direction of momentum. The skater leans inward, often touching the ground with gloved hands to balance the slide.

stalefish. While in mid-air, the skater grabs the board heelside and between his or her feet by reaching behind his or her body. Additionally, the skater pivots so that knees and hips are facing in the direction of the board.

stalls. Creating a dramatic pause by holding a trick still before continuing the run. Often done after ollieing onto a structure.

switch stance. Riding the board with footing opposite from what is normal for that rider. If a rider's normal stance is regular foot than the switch stance is goofyfoot and vice versa.

tailslide. Sliding the underside of the tail end of a board on a ledge or lip.

tweek. When skateboarder grabs the board to add a twist to a particular trick.

varial. The skateboarder spins 180 degrees but the board does not.

types of skateboarding

longboarding. Skateboarding that does not emphasize getting air; instead, the longer board (usually 38 inches or more) is used for downhill speed and slalom or for flatland cruising and transportation. Additionally, some surf moves are used such as "dancing" on the board, which requires the rider to gracefully move up and down along the board while in motion as well as stand up paddling, which entails propelling the board by using a paddle instead of pushing with one's feet.

skate plaza.   A park that is constructed to imitate ordinary street obstacles. Rob Dyrdek has promoted these types of parks to support street skating. These manufactured plazas are used in street competitions.

street skating.   Skating that emphasizes getting air. Frequently tricks are performed on streets, curbs, benches, handrails, and other elements of urban and suburban landscapes.

vert skating.   Skating on ramps and other vertical structures specifically designed for skating.

  half pipe.   A U-shaped ramp of any size, usually with a flat section in the middle.

  vert ramp.   A half pipe, usually at least 8 feet tall, with steep sides that are perfectly vertical near the top.

  megaramp.   A nine-story tall and over 100-yard long ramp. It is composed of two main parts. The initial ramp and jump lead to a 70-foot gap and end with a 27-foot vertical ramp. These are featured in Big Air competitions and in the many feats of Danny Way.

  bowl.   Any variation of riding surface that looks like an empty swimming pool. Bowls can be concrete or made from wood. The Pro-tec pool party that is hosted at the Vans indoor park features top bowl skaters.

skateboard jargon

bail.   When a skater chooses to abandon a trick in progress because he or she perceives himself or herself unable to complete it. Often done to avoid serious injury.

bombing a hill.   When longboarders skate downhill for speed; top speeds have been clocked at 60 miles per hour.

gnarly.   Used to emphasize an extraordinary level of unexpected behavior or to describe the unexpected nature of an object. Can have either positive or negative connotations.

land a trick. When a skater successfully completes a trick by landing with both feet on the board and in control of the board.

sick. An adjective that signifies the positive; essentially, sick means good. Similar to the word *cool*, it can be used to positively affirm a variety of things such as a sick trick or a sick skate park. Similarly, the word *ill* can be used to designate something that is cool.

sketchy. An activity, such as a skate trick, that is not well done. Or a person's behavior that is not trustworthy.

stoked. To be very excited about or energized by something.

main references for terminology

Cave, Steve. (n.d.). Skateboarding dictionary: glossary of skateboarding words and terms. Retrieved from http://skateboard.about.com/od/ skateboardingdictionary/Skateboarding_Dictionary_Glossary_of _Skateboarding_Words_and_Terms.htm.

Definition of skate tricks and terms. (n.d.). Retrieved from http://www .ramprage.com/forums/f56/definitions-skate-trick-terms-13799/.

Skateboarding glossary. (n.d.). Retrieved from http://www.exploratorium .edu/skateboarding/largeglossary.html.

Skateboard tricktionary. (n.d.). Retrieved from http://www.board -crazy.co.uk/tricktionary.php.

bibliography

"About." (n.d.). *RobDyrdek.com*. Retrieved from http://www.dyrdek.com/index.php?c=html&s=more&id=31.

"All about." (n.d.). *BobBurnquist.com*. Retrieved from http://www.bobburnquist.com/index.php?page=about.

Annobil, K. (2009, March 22). "Stevie Williams." Retrieved from http://www.formatmag.com/features/stevie-williams/.

Atencio, M., & Beal, B. (2011). "Beautiful Losers": The symbolic exhibition and legitimization of outsider masculinity. *Sport and Society, 14*, 1–16.

Atencio, M., Beal, B., & Wilson C. (2009). Distinction of risk: Urban skateboarding, street habitus, and the construction of hierarchical gender relations. *Qualitative Research in Sport and Exercise, 1*, 3–20.

Badenhausen, K. (2009, February 18). "The highest-paid action sports stars." Retrieved from http://www.forbes.com/2009/02/17/shaun-white-tony-hawk-business-sports_0218_action_sports.html.

Beal, B. (1995). Disqualifying the official: An exploration of social resistance in the subculture of skateboarding. *Sociology of Sport Journal, 12*, 252–267.

Beal, B., & Weidman, L. (2003). Authenticity in the skateboarding world. In R. Rinehart & S. Sydnor (Eds.), *To the Extreme: Alternative Sports, Inside and Out* (pp. 337–352). New York: SUNY Press.

Beal, B., & Wilson, C. (2004). "Chicks dig scars": Transformations in the subculture of skateboarding. In B. Wheaton (Ed.), *Understanding*

Lifestyle Sports: Consumption, Identity, and Difference (pp. 31–54). London: Routledge Press.

Beato, G. (1999, March). The lords of Dogtown. *Spin.* Retrieved from http://angelfire.com/ca/alva3/spin.html

Bennett, G., & Lachowetz, T. (2004). Marketing to lifestyles: Action sports and Generation Y. *Sport Marketing Quarterly, 13,* 239–243.

Binelli, Mark. (2008, August 7). Eighty-eight acres of anarchy in the USA. *Rolling Stone, 1058,* 43–51.

"Bio." (n.d.). *RodneyMullen.net.* Retrieved from http://www.rodney mullen.net/bio.html

Borden, I. (2001). *Skateboarding, Space, and the City: Architecture and the Body.* Oxford: Berg.

Branch, J. (2010, May 14). To fix bridge, skateboard mecca may be lost. *New York Times,* B11.

Brisick, J. (2010, December 12). Wrestling elephants. *At Home with: Stacy Peralta.* Retrieved from http://jamiebrisick.com/2010/12/12/ at-home-with-stacy-peralta/

Brooke, M. (1999). *The Concrete Wave: The History of Skateboarding.* Toronto: Warwick Publishing.

Browne, D. (2004). *Amped: How Big Air, Big Dollars, and a New Generation Took Sports to the Extreme.* New York: Bloomsbury.

Browne, D. (2005, June 5). Dogtown East. *New York Magazine.* Retrieved from http://nymag.com/print/?/nymetro/news/sports/features/11956

"Burnside skatepark: Portland's famous skatepark." (n.d.). Retrieved from http://www.uniquely-portland-oregon.com/burnside-skatepark.html

"Cara-Beth Burnside." (n.d.). *The Woman of Action Network.* Retrieved from http://www.woa.tv/articles/at_cara-beth_burnside.html

Chiu, Chihsin. (2009). Contestation and conformity: Street and park skateboarding in New York City public space. *Space and Culture, 12,* 25–42.

Chivers Yochim, E. (2010). *Skate Life: Re-Imaging White Masculinity.* Ann Arbor: University of Michigan Press.

Christian, M. (2010, April 14). "We're looking for our next group of young entrepreneurs. Are you one?" Retrieved from http://www .ebonyjet.com/Templates/DetailsView.aspx?id=16820&terms =Stevie%20Williams

Clemmitt, M. (2009, April 9). Extreme sports: Are they too dangerous? *CQ Researcher, 19*(13), 297–320.

Corbett, S. (March 2000). The unbearable lightness of being the boarder queen. *Outside*, 64–68, 131, 134, 135, 138.

Curiel, Jonathan. (2011, February 5). Tommy Guerrero: The skateboarder with the music touch. Retrieved from http://www.kqed.org/arts/music/article.jsp?essid=43150

Dang, K. (2008 July 2). Lifers: Generations of skateboarders keep rolling. *Boise Weekly*. Retrieved from http://www.boiseweekly.com/boise/lifers/Content?oid=937239

Daugherty, C. (2008, December 11). Questions for: Danny Way. *Wall Street Journal*. Retrieved from http://online.wsj.com/article/SB122894639433295903.html

Davidson, B. (1976). *The Skateboard Book*. New York: Grosset & Dunlap.

Davidson, J. (1985). Sport and modern technology: The rise of skateboarding, 1963–1978. *Journal of Popular Culture, 18*(4), 145–157.

Davis, J. (1999). *Skateboard Roadmap*. London, UK: Carlton Books Ltd.

Deberdt, B. (2011, March 11). Tommy Guerrero: here and now. *Huck, 25*. Retrieved from http://www.huckmagazine.com/features/tommy-guerrero/

"Definition of skate tricks and terms." (n.d.). Retrieved from http://www.ramprage.com/forums/f56/definitions-skate-trick-terms-13799/

Deford, F. (1977, February 7). Promo wiz in kidvid biz. *Sports Illustrated*, 30–33. Retrieved from http://sportsillustrated.cnn.com/vault/article/magazine/MAG1092029/index.htm

Dehaas, J. (2010, October 11). Fans say it's eco-friendly, cops say it's risky. The fight over longboarding. *Maclean's, 123*(39), 69–70.

Dinces, S. (2011) "Flexible opposition": Skateboarding subcultures under the rubric of late capitalism. *International Journal of the History of Sport, 28*(11), 1512–1535.

Dougherty, C. (2009, February 27). Skateboarding tourney stirs its own midnight madness. *Wall Street Journal*. Retrieved from http://online.wsy.com/article/SB123568608719787029.html

Dumas, A., & Laforest, S. (2009). Skateparks as health resource: Are they as dangerous as they look? *Leisure Studies, 28*, 19–34.

Edgers, G. (2002, June 16). The 250 million skate punk extreme sportsman Tony Hawk soars over a pop culture empire. *Boston Globe*, L1.

Egan, J. (1998, April). Girl over board. *Sports for Women*, 133–135, 166.

Ellick, A. (2009, January 26). Skateboarding in Afghanistan provides a diversion form desolation. *New York Times*. Retrieved from http://www.nytimes.com/2009/01/26/sports/othersports/26skate.html

Fisher, E. (2011, July 12). PAS house: Pierre-Andre Senizergue's completely skateable home in Malibu. *Huffington Post*. Retrieved from http://www.huffingtonpost.com/2011/07/12/pas-house-a-skate boarders_n_896310.html

Freedman, J. (Producer), & Montano, C. (Director). (2006). *Rising Son: The Legend of Skater Christian Hosoi* [motion picture]. United States: QD3 Entertainment and Quiksilver.

Gabriel, T. (1987, July 16–30). Rolling thunder. *Rolling Stone, 504/505*, 73–76.

Glader, P. (2007, July 27). Avid boarders bypass branded gear—the $15 "blank decks" work just fine: A marketing challenge for the industry. *Wall Street Journal*, B1.

Gonzalez, K., (2011, June 6). X Games history 1990s to 2011 and the high dollar draw of pro skateboarding. *Yahoo! Sports*. Retrieved from http://sports.yahoo.com/top/news?slug=ycn-8591851

Gonzalez, K. (2011, July 7). The Hood Games exhibit opens July 15th at the AAACC in San Francisco, California. *Yahoo! Sports*. Retrieved from http://sports.yahoo.com/top/news?slug=ycn -8763267

Greenfeld, K. (2004, June 7). Skate and destroy. *Sports Illustrated, 100* (23), 66–80.

Hamm, K. (2011, November 30). Montreal's Big O moved but preserved. Retrieved from http://espn.go.com/espn/print?id=7298058 &type=HeadlineNews&

Heizer, C. (2004). Street smarts. *Parks & Recreation, 39*(11), 74–79.

Heywood, L. (2006). Producing girls: Empire, sport, and the neoliberal body. In J. Hargreaves & P. Vertinsky (Eds.), *Physical Culture, Power, and the Body* (pp. 101–120). London: Routledge.

Higgins, M. (2006, July 26). Skateboarding: On a mission, and rolling. *New York Times*. Retrieved from http://query.nytimes.com/gst/ fullpage.html?res=9904E5D9153FF935A15754C0A9609C8

Higgins, M. (2006, November 1). A skateboarding ramp reaches for the sky. *New York Times*. Retrieved from http://www.nytimes.com/ 2006/11/01/sports/othersports/01ramp.html

Higgins, M. (2007, June 6). Riders of the world, unite! Skateboading sprouts as team sport. *New York Times*. Retrieved from http:// www.nytimes.com/2007/06/06/sports/othersports/06skate.html

Higgins, M. (2007, June 14). IOC woos skateboarding. *New York Times*. Retrieved from http://www.nytimes.com/2007/06/14/sports/14iht -OLY.1.6135217.html

Higgins, M. (2009, July 29). Stepping aside as his creation soars. *New York Times*. Retrieved from http://www.nytimes.com/2009/07/30/ sports/30xgames.html

Higgins, M. (2010, May 26). The Shredder's Liberation army. *ESPN.com*. Retrieved from http://sports.espn.go.com/espn/print?id=5223304 &type=story

Higgins, M. (2010, July 20). Skateboarding glides into new phase. *New York Times*. Retrieved from http://www.nytimes.com/2010/07/21/ sports/21longboard.html?_r=2&ref=sports

Higgins, M. (2010, October 15). Dew, Maloofs talk skate comps for '11. *ESPN Action Sports*. Retrieved from https://m.espn.go.com/ wireless/story?storyId=5688324

Higgins, M. (2011, May 13). X Games to expand to six events in 2013. *ESPN Action Sports*. Retrieved from http://sports.espn.go.com/ action/news/story?id=6553598

Holthouse, D. (2007, August 9). Ghetto superstar. *Rolling Stone, 1032*, 82–86.

Horelick, M. (2007, November 18). Board out of their minds. *Los Angeles Times*. Retrieved from http://articles.latimes.com/2007/nov/18/ sports/sp-signalhill18

Howell, O. (2003). Extreme market research: Tales from the underbelly of skater-cool. *Topic, 4*. Retrieved from http://www.webdelsol.com ?topoic?articles?04/howell.html

Howell, O. (2005). The "creative class" and the gentrifying city: Skateboarding in Philadelphia's Love Park. *Journal of Architectural Education, 59*(2), 32–42.

Howell, O. (2008). Skate park as neoliberal playground: Urban governance, recreation space, and cultivation of personal responsibility. *Space and Culture, 11*, 475–496.

Hyman, M. (2006, November 13). How Tony Hawk stays aloft. *Business Week, 4009*, 84–88.

Iwata, E. (2008, March 10). Tony Hawk leaps to top of financial empire. *USA Today*, 1B.

Johnston, B. A. (2010, July 28). Danny Way and the gift of fear. *Men's Journal*. Retrieved from http://www.mensjournal.com/danny-way

Kane, Rich. (2010, June 22). Duane's addictions: Skateboarding, punk rock, drugs, tattoos, sobriety. *OC Weekly, 21*. Retrieved from http://duanepeters.net/articles-press/o-c-weekly-from-a-decade-back -fuckin-a-time-dont-stay/ (reprint)

Kellett, P., & Russell R. (2009). A comparison between mainstream and action sport industries in Australia: A case study of the skateboarding cluster. *Sport Management Review, 12*, 66–78.

Kelly, M. L. (2010, October 29). Tony Hawk: From skateboard misfit to CEO. *National Public Radio*. Retrieved from http://www.npr.org/ templates/transcript/transcipt.php?story Id=130859155

Krasny, M. (2011, April 18). First person: Tommy Guerrero. Retrieved from http://www.kqed.org/a/forum/R201104181000

Lannes, X. (2010, January 19). Lyn-Z Hawkins for I skate therefore I am . . . the interview. Retrieved from http://poolrider.blogspot.com/ 2010/01/lyn-z-hawkins-for-i-skate-therefore-i.html

Lannes, X. (2010, November 7). Patti McGee 1965 skateboard champion. Retrieved from http://poolrider.blogspot.com/2010/11/patti-mcgee -1965-skateboard-champion.html

Lannes, X. (2011, January 6). Jim Fitzpatrick interview: I skate therefore I am. Retrieved from http://poolrider.blogspot.com/2011/01/ jim-fitzpatrick-interview-part-ii-1957.html

Layden, T. (2002, June 10). What is this 34-year-old man doing on a skateboard? Making millions. *Sports Illustrated*, 80.

Levine, M. (1999, July 26). The Birdman. *New Yorker*, 68–77.

Levy, D. (2003, February). Interview: Cesario "Block" Montano. *Juice, 56*. Retrieved from http://www.juicemagazine.com/BLOCK.html

Libes, H. (2003, February 2). Stacy Peralta's next wave. *Los Angeles Times*. Retrieved from http://articles.latimes.com/2003/feb/02/magazine/tm-peralta05

Loew, T. (2008, June 19). Skateboarding kick-flips its way into PE classes. *USA Today, Life*, 7D.

Lucero, J. (Director). (2005). *Who Cares: The Duane Peters Story*. [motion picture] United States: Black Label Pictures.

"Lyn-Z Adams Hawkins." (n.d.). Retrieved from http://www.woa.tv/articles/at_lyn-z_adams_hawkins.html

MacKaye, I. (n.d.). Duane Peters. *Juice, 58*. Retrieved from http://www.juicemagazine.com/duanepetersianmackaye.html

McGee, P. (2009). 1st Betty. In J. Smith (Ed), *Lives on Board* (pp. 323–324). Morrow Bay, CA: Morrow Skateboard Group.

McReynolds, D. (2008, January 15). Q & A with skateboarder Rodney Mullen. *Daily Bruin*. Retrieved from http://www.dailybruin.com/index.php/article/2008/01/q-skateboarder-rodney-mullen

Montgomery, T. (2009, May 12). The state of the skateboarding industry. Retrieved from http://www.shop-eat-surf.com/news-item/914/state-of-skateboarding-industry

Mortimer, S. (2008). *Stalefish: Skateboard Culture from the Rejects Who Made It*. San Francisco: Chronicle Books.

National Sporting Goods Association. (2008). Skateboarding 10-year winner in sports participation growth. *Press release*. Retrieved from http:www.nsga.org/i4a/pages/index.cfm?pageid=3966

Nealon, S. (2009, May 29). Inland skateboarders use growing national association to strut their stuff. *Press Enterprise*. Retrieved from http://www.pe.com/localnesw/morenovalley/stories/PE_News_Local_s_skate30.3620d9b

Netravali, A. (2008). Biodegradable composites make eco-friendly skateboards—and create local jobs. *Human Ecology, 36*, 24.

Nieratko, C. (2009, February 13). Enter the Berrics. Retrieved from http://espn.go.com/espn/print?id=3906007&type

Nieratko, C. (2011, March 15). Tampa Pro: Nieratko's take. *ESPN.com*. Retrieved from http://espn.go.com/action/skateboarding/news/story?page=2011-tampa-pro-nieratko

Nieratko, C. (2011, November 10). The Nyjah Huston interview. *Skateboarder*. 71–77.

Norcross, D. (2006, August 24). Wonder Woman: Action icon Cara-Beth Burnside always has been a mover and a shaker. *San Diego Union*. Retrieved from http://www.signonsandiego.com/uniontrib/20060824/news_lz1s24wonder.html

Oksana. (2011, July 8). Spain's teenager playground–the Factoria Joven. Retrieved from http://urbanpeek.com/2011/07/08/joven/

O'Mahoney, J. (n.d.). Laura Thornhill. *Juice, 65*. Retrieved from http://www.juicemagazine.com/LAURATHORNHILL.html

Owen, A. (2000, Winter). Cara-Beth Burnside: how to burn the candle at both ends. *Wahine, 6*(1), 48–49, 54.

Pickert, K. (2009, January 22). The X Games. *Time*. Retrieved from http://www.time.com/time/nation/article/0,8599,1873166,00.html

"Pinball skatepark built in New Zealand." (2011, June 4). Retrieved from http://www.caughtinthecrossfire.com/skate/skate-news/pinball-skatepark-built-in-new-zealand/

Pomerantz, S., Currie, D. H. & Kelly, D. M. (2004). Sk8er girls: Skateboarding, girlhood, and feminism on the move. *Women's Studies International Forum, 27*, 547–557.

Porter, N. (2003). Female skateboarders and their negotiation of space and identity, *Journal for Arts, Sciences, and Technology, 1*, 75–80.

Putnam, B. (2006, July 25). SPoT has made its mark on the world of skateboarding. *St. Petersburg Times*, 1C, 8C.

Quiksilver. (2002, June 26). Quiksilver launches Quiksilver entertainment: Riding wave of brand consumer interest on actins sports lifestyle. *Press Release*. Retrieved from biz.yahoo.com/prnews/020626/sfw067a_1.html

Rinehart, R. (2005). "Babes" & boards: Opportunities in new millennium sport? *Journal of Sport and Social Issues, 29*, 232–255.

Rinehart, R., & Grenfell, C. (2002). BMX spaces: Children's grass roots' courses and corporate-sponsored tracks. *Sociology of Sport Journal, 19*, 302–314

"Rodney Mullen." (n.d.). *Grind TV*. Retrieved from http://www.grindtv .com/athlete/rodney-mullen/biography

Roope, J. (2011, May 11) Skaters train "illegally" for growing sport. Retrieved from http://www.cnn.com/2011/US/05/11/skateboard racing/index.html

Rubial, S. (2008, July 9). Hawk's Jam to hit the road. *USA Today*, 10.

Siler, R. (2003, August 10). X Games' labor pains: Skateboarders seek more prize money, improved conditions. *Daily News*. Retrieved from http://www.thefreelibrary.com/X+Games+Labor+Pains +Skateboarders+Seek+More+Prize+Money,+Improved. . .-a010 6497397

"Skateboard tricktionary." (n.d.). Retrieved from http://www.board -crazy.co.uk/tricktionary.php

Skateistan. (n.d.). "Our story." Retrieved from http://skateistan.org/ content/our-story

Skyler, B. (2007, October 19). The wheel deal, part 2. *eXtreme Sports Physics*. Rctricvcd from http://extremesportsphysics.blogspot.com/ 2007/10/wheel-deal-part-2-wheel-size-again.html

Stevens, C. (2002, November 6). The father of pro-skateboarding: Skateboard pioneer takes it easy in Boise. *Boise Weekly*. Retrieved from http://www.skatewhat.com/russhowell/WebPage-Biography -BoiseWeekly.html

Tesler, P. (2007, May 4). Ramp it up. *Current Science*, *92*, 4–7.

Tesler, P., & Doherty, P. (n.d.). Frontside forces and fakie flight: The physics of skateboarding tricks. *San Francisco Exploratorium*. Retrieved from http://www.exploratorium.edu/skateboarding/trick .html

"The Berrics with Pro Skater & Entrepreneur Steve Berra." Retrieved from http://www.malakye.com/asp/front/CMSPage.asp?TYP _ID=2&ID=2421

Thornhill, L. (2009). Some golden times in my years on the magic rolling board. In J. Smith (Ed.), *Lives on Board* (pp. 318–319). Morro Bay, CA: Morro Skateboard Group.

Thorpe, H., & Wheaton, B. (2011). The Olympic movement: Action sports and the search for Generation Y. In J. Sugden & A. Tomlinson (Eds.), *Watching the Olympics: Politics, Power and Representation* (pp. 182–200). London: Routledge.

Tony Hawk Foundation. (n.d.). Why are skateparks beneficial to communities? Retrieved from http://www..tonyhawkfoundation.org/faq

Valentine, G. (1996). Children should be seen and not heard: the production and transgression of adults' public space, *Urban Geography, 15*, 205–220.

Verdon, J. (2009, July). Skateboard retailers take a leap. *Record: North Jersey.com*. Retrieved from http://www.northjersey.com/news/business/Skateboard_retailers_take_a_leap.html

Verhgese, M. (n.d.). La Facotria Joven. Retrieved from http://www.iconeye.com/news/news/la-factoria-joven

Vivoni, F. (2009). Sports of spatial desires: Skateparks, skateplazas, and urban politics. *Journal of Sport and Social Issues, 33*, 130–149.

Walk, S. (2006) Presidential Keynote Address, presented at the annual meeting of the North American Society for the Sociology of Sport, Vancouver, British Columbia.

Wanner, N. (n.d.). The science and art of skateboard design. *San Francisco Exploratorium*. Retrieved from http://www.exploratorium.edu/skateboarding/skatedesign.html

Weyland, J. (2002). *The answer is never: A skateboarder's history of the world*. New York: Grove Press.

Wheaton, Belinda. (2005). Selling out? The commercialization and globalization of lifestyle sport. In L. Allison (Ed.), *The Global Politics of Sport: The Role of Global Institutions in Sport* (pp. 140–185). London: Routledge.

Wheaton, B. (forthcoming). *Lifestyle sport: The cultural politics of alternative sports*. London: Routledge.

Wheaton, B., & Beal, B. (2003). "Keeping it real": Subcultural media and the discourses of authenticity in alternative sport. *International Review for the Sociology of Sport, 38*, 155–176.

Willard, M. N. (1998). Séance, tricknowlogy, skateboarding, and the space of youth. In J. Austin & M. N. Willard (Eds.), *Generations of Youth: Youth Cultures and History in Twentieth-Century America* (pp. 327–346). New York: New York University Press.

Willis, C. (n.d.). The real story: At least my story. Retrieved from http://www.burnsideproject.blogspot.com/

Wilson, B. (2010 August 25). Street skateboarding goes big with $1.2M tour. http://www.eastvalleytribune.com/local/the_valley/article _36e84070-b08f-11df-8690-001cc4c03286.html

Wise, M. (2002, August 18). X Games: Skateboarders landing in the real world. *New York Times*. Retrieved from http://www.nytimes.com/ 2002/08/18/sports/x-games-skateboarders-are-landing-in-real -world.html?

Woolley, H., Hazelwood, T., & Simkins, I. (2011). Don't skate here: The exclusion of skateboarders from urban civic spaces in three northern cities in England. *Journal of Urban Design, 16*, 471–487.

Yoshiura, M. (n.d.). Christian Hosoi: A born-again Christian. *Transition: You Are in Control Hawaii*. Retrieved from http://www.transition hawaii.com/community/around_the_islands/features/christian _hosoi

Zitzer, P. (2010 March). Timeline: Vanessa Toress. *Skateboard, 73*, 52, 58, 62. Retrieved from http://www.skatergirl.co.uk/wp-content/ uploads/2010/02/vanessa-timeline-1small.jpg

index

1976 Olympics, 48
1995 Slam City Jam, 82
1998 Winter Olympics, 76
1999 X Games, 56
2009 X Games, 76
360 Degrees in a Full Pipe, 68
540 McTwist (First), 85, 87
7 Fingers Production, 49
7 Ply Maple Boards, 92, 94
900, Tony Hawk's, 56, 74; on MegaRamp, 82
900 Films, 75

ABC (Television Network), 10–11, 15
ABC's *Wide World of Sports*, 11
About A Boy (Novel by Nick Hornby), 38
Academy of Skateboard Film Makers, Arts and Sciences, 104
Action Figures, 79
Action Now (Magazine), 19
Action Sports Alliance, 40, 104
Action Sports Environmental Coalition, 76, 87, 106
Activision (Videogame Company), 32, 74
Adaptation, 27

Adaptive Action Sports, 39
Adams, Jay, 14, 65
Adidas, 3, 38
Adult Supervision, 101
The Aerial, 15
Aesthetics, 28
Affoumado, Jaime, 50
African Americans in Skateboarding, 17, 51, 83, 84
Air Resistance, 92, 97
Airwalk (Brand), 73
AKA: Skater Girl (Movie), 85
Alba, Steve, 68
All Girl Skate Jam, 29–30, 71, 76, 101; history of, 54; incorporation into WarpTour; 39
Allie Sports, 37, 56
All-Pro Skateboard Cards, 18
Almost Skateboards, 69–70
Alter, Hobie, 9
Altered State, 41
Alternative Image, 103
Alva, Tony, 14, 25, 65, 72, 75
Amateur Status, 53
Amazing Square, 48
American Skateboard Championships (1965), 10
Anaheim, California, United States, 11, 84

Angular Momentum, 95
ANP (Artists Network Project), 50
ANP Quarterly (Magazine),
    51, 104
Anti-Establishment. *See*
    Skateboarding Ethos
Anti-Hero (Brand), 50
Anti-Skate Devices, 100
The Aquabats (Musical Group), 41
Arizona Pipes, 66
Art in the Street (Art Exhibit), 51
Artistic Expression, 30
Artwork, 49
Artzine, 50
Asian Americans in
    Skateboarding, 17
Assembly Bill 1296, 33
Australia, 2, 25
Australian Short Board
    Surfers, 17
Axel (Trucks), 91

Back to the Banks
    (Competition), 45
Back to the Future (Movie), 25
Bahne (Company), 13
Ball Bearings, 93
Balma, Larry, 20
Barbee, Ray, 24, 50, 80
Barcelona, 48
Battle at the Berrics, 47, 48
Battle of the Network Stars
    (Television Show), 19
Bay Area, California, United
    States, 52
Bearer, Danny, 9
Bearer, Wendy, 10
Beastie Boys, 24, 72
Beatnik Termites, 41

Beautiful Losers
    (Art Exhibit), 32, 51
Beijing, China, 52
Being John Malkovich (Movie), 27
Bench Utilization, 45
Berkeley, California, United
    States, 58
Berra, Steve, 47
Berrics, 47
Big Air, 96; controversy, 56
Big Brother (Magazine),
    22, 25, 27
Big O, 48
Birdhouse (Brand), 74
Black Pearl (World's Largest
    Skate Park), 2, 48
Blender, Neil, 20
Blind (Company), 26
Blink-182 (Musical Group), 49
Blktop Project, 50
Block, Ken, 78
BMX Biking, 36, 52
Bones Brigade, 25, 26, 65, 73, 97
Bones Brigade Video Show, 24
"Born to Skate" (Song), 41
Bostick, Danielle, 22, 33
Bostick, Don, 22, 33
Boston, Massachusetts, United
    States, 36
Bowls, 96
Boyd, Colleen, 11
Branch, John, 45
Branker, Don, 18
Brazil, 2
Bricks, 54
Brittain, Grant, 20, 104
Brolin, Josh, 25
The Brooke Institute, 71
Brooklyn Banks, 45

Brooklyn Bridge, 45
Brown, Jake, 56, 96
Bufoni, Leticia, 41
Burnquist, Bob, 33, 59, 88, 96;
   biography of, 82–83
Burnquist, Jasmyn, 83
Burnquist, Lotus, 83
Burnquist, Veronica Nachard, 83
Burnquist, Vitoria, 83
Burnside Bridge, 43, 104;
   history of, 44; tax-exempt
   organization, 44
Burnside, Cara-Beth "C. B.," 22,
   33, 40, 41, 71; biography of,
   75–76

Caballero, Steve, 24
Cable, Wisconsin, 52
Cadillac Wheels, 12, 13
Cal Jam II, 18, 49, 67
Calgary, Alberta, Canada, 48
California African American
   Museum, 51
California Amateur Skateboard
   League, 22, 73
California High School
   Skateboard Club, 36
California Skateboard
   Association, 19
Camp Kill Yourself (CKY), 37.
   See also Jackass
Camp Pendleton, 16
Camp Woodward, history of, 52
Campbell, Kareem, 33
Canada, 2, 57
Canadian Amateur Skateboarding
   Association, 37
Cannon, Don, 84
Caron, Amy, 85

Cash, Donna, 10
Caswell, Laura Thornhill. *See*
   Thornhill, Laura
Cayman Islands, 2
Cemetery of Reason (Book), 49
Cendali, Richard, 35
Central Park, 51
Centripetal Force, 96
Charlie's Angels, 65
Cheer, 52
Chica Rider, 39
Chicago Roller Skate
   Company, 10
China, 2, 54
Christ Air, 71
Circle Jerks, 24
Clark, Larry, 38
Clash, 68
Code 13, 41
Cole, Chris, 40
Commercialism, 3
Conflict with Government
   Officials, 46
Consumer Reports (Magazine), 11
Contests, 53
Copenhagen, Denmark, 50
Copper Mountain (Colorado), 52
Corporations, 104
CreateaSkate (Educational
   Curriculum), 35
Creative Ethos, 43, 101
*Crips and Bloods: Made in
   America* (Movie), 66
CSI: Miami (Television Show), 50

The Daffy (Technique), 15
Dal Santo, Leticia, 41
Dallas, Texas, United States, 66
Damn Am, 54

Davis, California, United States, 89

DC MegaRamp, 87. *See also* MegaRamp

DC Shoes, 52, 78, 79, 83

Deck, 91

Decline in Skateboarding in the Late 1970s, 19

Deformer (2008), 50

Del Mar (California) Skateboard Championships (1975), 17

Deluxe Distribution, 50

Designs (of Skateboards), 91–94

Dew Tour, 36, 40, 56

Diameter of Wheels, 93

Dias, Sandro, 41

Dirty Ghetto Kids (DGK), 84

Disney Corporation, 31, 39, 55

Dogtown and Z-Boys (Movie), 7, 14, 38, 64, 72, 104

Doherty, Paul, 92, 97

Do-It-Yourself (DIY) Ethos, 4, 24, 43, 47, 49, 66, 106, 107

Dominican Republic, 35

Downhill Motion (Movie), 17

Downhill Skaters, 15, 39. *See also* Longboarding

"Downtown Is Dogtown" (Song), 41

Durban, South Africa, 2

Durometer, 93

Drop into Skateboarding (organization), 3

Dyrdek, Rob, 7, 46, 57, 104; biography of, 79–80

Dyrdek Foundation, 57, 104

E-Commerce, 37

Early Skateboards, 9, 10

Ebony (Magazine), 83

Edmunds, Marc "Ali," 50

Educate to Skate, 84

Element, 85, 89

The Endless Summer (Movie), 10

Energy Flow and Transfer, 94

Engblom, Skip, 16, 65

Environmentalism, 106. *See also* Action Sports Environmental Coalition

Escalera (Musical Group), 78

ESPN (Television Network), sponsor of the X Games: 3, 31, 39, 46, 55, 74, 76, 107

ESPN Boycott Threat, 40

ESPN2 (Television Network), 31

Ethnic Diversity, 17

Etnies, 80, 105

Europe, 25

The European Cup, 25

European Skateboard Association, 36

Extreme Games. *See* X Games

"Extreme" Promotion, 4, 32

The Faction (Musical Group), 41

Factoria Joven, 106

Fast-Food Industry, 107

Female Equity Issues, 22, 30, 40, 101; media exposure, 55; pay, 76

Fever Pitch (book by Nick Hornby), 38

Fiasco, Lupe (Hip-Hop Artist), 2

Fibreflexes (Brand), 10

Firm (Company), 26

First Betty (Brand), 62

First Skate Park (Florida), 18

Fitzpatrick, Jim, 9, 40; biography, 62–63
Flanagan, Pat, 18
Flexibility, 94
Fort Myers, Florida, United States, 80
Foucault, Michael, 100
Foundation (Company), 26
Fox, Michael J., 25
France, 48
Free Beer (Musical Group), 50
Free Former (Brand), 66
Freedom Ethos, 43, 49
Freestyle, Aerial Evolution, 21
Freewheelin' (Movie), 18, 65
Fries, John, 9
Frontslide 180, physics of the, 95
Fu Manchu (Musical Group), 41
FuelTV, 52
Funny or Die, 75
Futura 2000, 50

G-Forces, 94
Gagnon, Pierre-Luc, 40
Gainesville, Florida, United States, 69
Garret, Leif, 18
Gasner, Eli, 51
Gatorade Free Flow Tour, 56
Geezerskates, 34
Gelfand, Alan, 21
Gender Norms, 100. *See also* Female Equity Issues
Germany, 35
Getting Nowhere Faster (Movie), 85
Ghent, Belgium, 49
Gigantic Skatepark Tour, 74

Girl and Chocolate Skateboards (Company), 26
Girl Riders Organization (GRO), 39, 101
The Girls' Skate Network, 39
Gleaming the Cube (Movie), 25, 66, 69
Global X, 55
Globalization, 2, 104
"Go Skate" (Song), 41
Gonzales, Mark, 21, 26, 30, 38, 51, 81
Good Housekeeping (Magazine), 11
Gordon, Larry, 9
Gradual Curves, 97
Graffiti, 50, 51
Grand Canyon, 83
Gravity Games, 56
Great Wall of China Jump, 7, 77
Greenfield, Karl, 3
Grimes, Marty, 17
Grundy, Guy, 15
Guerrero, Tommy, 4, 24, 50
The Guinness Book of World Records, 15

Half Pipe, 76
Hammerhead Board, 72, 92
Handrail Utilization, 21, 45
Hardness of Wheel, 92–93
Harward, Bill, 12
Hawaii, 72
Hawk, Frank, 22, 73
Hawk, Keegan, 75
Hawk, Pat, 74
Hawk, Riley, 75
Hawk, Spencer, 75

Hawk, Tony, 1–2, 7, 21–22, 24–26, 33, 57, 59, 68, 71; biography of, 73–75
Hawk Clothing, 74
Hawkins-Pastrana, Lyn-Z Adams, 41, 96; biography of, 85–87
"Heaven Is a Half Pipe" (Song), 41
Heckler (Magazine), 27
"Hell Tours," 22
Hensley, Matt, 80
Hermosa, California, United States 10
Hitchcock, Garrison, 15
Ho, Jeff, 16, 65
Hobie Skateboards, 61, 66
Hoffman, Patty, 75
Hood Games Xperience, 52
Hornby, Nick, 38
Hosoi, Christian, 21, 23, 25; biography of, 71–73
Hosoi Skates, 23, 72
House of Vans, 38
How We Roll (Art Exhibit), 51
Howard, Rick, 26
Howell, Russ, 19; biography of, 63–64
The Hunns, 68
Huntington Beach, California, United States, 73
Huston, Adeyemi, 89
Huston, Kelle, 89
Huston, Nyjah, 40; biography of, 87–89
Hynson, Mike, 10

I & I (Brand), 89
IMG, 57
Independent (Company), 25

Indonesia Skateboarder Association, 37
Inline Skating, 52
Inner-City Neighborhoods, 52
Instructor Certifications, 19
Insurance Issues, 19. *See also* Legal Status
International Association of Skateboard Companies (IASC), 32, 34, 62, 63, 104
International Girl Skateboarding Association (IGSA), 71
International Go Skate Day, 104
International Gravity Sports Association (IGSA), 33, 58
International Hall of Fame, 82, 104
International Olympic Committee (IOC), 2, 36, 63, 103
International Professional Skateboard Association (IPSA), 19
International Skateboard Association (ISA), 18
International Skateboarding Day (June 21), 33
International Skateboarding Federation (ISF), 36
Irvine, California, United States, 84

Jackass (Television Show), 2, 27, 37
Japan, 25
Jan and Dean (Musical Group), 41
Jax (Musical Group), 68
Jefferson Starship (Musical Group), 41

Jet Black Crayon (Musical Group), 50
Jetton, Tony, 18, 70
JFA (Musical Group), 41
Johnson, Torger, 9
Jonze, Spike, 27

Kabul, Afghanistan, 2
Kalis, Josh, 83
Kaupas, Natas, 21
Kennedy, Terry, 79
Kessler, Andy, 50
Kettering, Ohio, United States, 46, 79
"Kick, Push" (Song), 41
Kickflip, 69
Kimberly, South Africa, 57
Kinetic Energy, 97
Klassen, Eric, 35
Knoop, Mimi, 40
Koston, Eric, 33, 47
Krause, Jessica, 29
Krooked (Brand), 50, 81
Krooked Grind, 93
Kubo, Shogo, 17, 72

La Faite Lyrique, 106
Laguna Beach, California, United States, 58
Lake Owen, 52
Larry Flint Publishers, 27
Las Vegas, Nevada, United States, 52, 57
Latino Skateboarders, 17
Lavigne, Avril, 2, 41
Legal Status, 32, 100. *See also* Assembly Bill 1296
Life (Magazine), 11, 61
Life of Ryan (Television Show), 2, 37

"Life on a Skateboard" (Song), 41
Lifeboats and Follies (Music Album), 50
Lives on Board (Book), 89
Local Skateboarding Scenes, 30
Logan, Bruce, 9
Logan Earth Ski, 67
London, England, United Kingdom, 48
Longboarding, 21, 39; events, 58
Los Angeles, California, United States, 46, 47
Los Angeles Times (Newspaper), 11
Love and Guts (Art Exhibit), 51
Love Park, 45, 83
Lyman, Kevin, 49

MacDonald, Andy, 33, 40
MacDonald, Jodi, 33
Madonna (Trick), 73
Magazines, 37
Mahoney, Jim, 19
Makaha Skateboards, 9, 62
Malibu, California, United States, 58, 106
Maloof Brothers, 57
Maloof Money Cup, 39, 40, 56, 103
Malto, Sean, 40
Management Disputes, 103
Margera, Bam, 37
Marketing, 7, 21
Marseille Skate Park, 48
Martin, Brewce, 44
Maryhill Festival of Speed, 58
Masculine Image, 30
Masters (Legends) Divisions, 34, 68

McDonalds, 3
McGee, Patti, 61
McKay, Colin, 78
Media, 23, 37
Media Technology, 97
MegaRamp, 52, 55, 77, 94;
    physics of, 96
Merida, Spain, 106
Meronek, Rob, 54
Michael Douglas Show
    (Television Show), 62
The Mighty Mama Skate-a-Rama
    Event, 38
Mini-Ramp, 39
Modesto, California, United
    States, 85
Momentum, 92
"Mondo Aggro" (Song), 41
Montreal, Canada, 48
Montreal Impact (Soccer Club), 48
Mothball (Artzine), 50
Mott, Tim, 80
Mountain, Lance, 24, 25, 26
Mountain Biking, 36
Mountain Dew, 3
Mt. Baldy, 16, 66
MTV (Television Network),
    2, 37, 79
Mujica, Ricky, 50
Mullen, Rodney, 21, 24;
    biography of, 69–70
Munster, Germany, 36
Murden, Barbara, 52
Museum of Contemporary Art–
    Barcelona, Spain (MACBA), 48
Museum of Contemporary Art–
    Los Angeles, 51
Music Inspired by
    Skateboarding, 41

Musical Influences, 24, 30
Muska, Chad, 33
"My Skateboard" (Song), 41
"My Soul Is Worried Not Me"
    (Song), 50

Nasworthy, Frank, 12, 13
National Basketball Association,
    39, 57
National High School Skateboard
    Association, 36
National Public Radio (NPR), 4
National Skateboarding
    Association (NSA), 22,
    33, 73
National Skateboarding
    Association of South
    Africa, 37
Native Americans in
    Skateboarding, 51
NBC (Television Network),
    3, 36, 56
NBC Sports, 37
Neiman, Leroy, 19
The Netherlands, 54
New York, New York, United
    States, 45, 50
Newport Beach, California,
    United States, 67
NHS's Road Riders, 13
Nieratko, Chris, 54
Nike, skateboard market, 3, 26,
    31, 38, 39; sponsorship, 36, 51,
    81, 104
Nike Skateboard Shoes, 31
Nils Staerk Gallery, 50
Nitro Circus Live, 87
NOFX (Musical Group), 41
Nollie (Technique), 93

Northern California Downhill
  Skateboarding Association, 58
Nose Design, 92–93
Nose Wheelie (Technique), 15
Nosegrind (Technique), 93
Noseslide (Technique), 93

Oakland, California, United
  States, 51, 52
Oakley (Brand), 51
O'Brien, Jen, 33, 40, 83
Oceanside, California, United
  States, 69
O'Dea, Tim, 77
Oki, Peggy, 17
Ollie, 21, 69; physics of, 94, 95
Olson, Steve, 68
The Olympics, 2, 36
O'Neal, Ellen, 18
OPM (Musical Group), 41
Orange, California, United States,
  46, 57, 75
Orange County, California, United
  States, 72
Organizational Disputes, 103

"Packaging" of the Skateboarding
  Lifestyle, 31, 37, 38, 49, 105
Page, Ty, 18
Paranoid Park (Movie), 38, 44
Parking Block Utilization, 21
Parkour, 106–107
Parks, Corey, 68
Participation Trends, 1, 38–39
PAS (Pierre-Andre Senizergues)
  Skateboarding House, 105
"Pass the Mic" (Song), 72
Pastrana, Travis, 87
Pennywise, 49

Pepsi Corporation, 18
Pepsi Pro Skateboard Team, 18
Peralta, Stacy, skateboarder, 14,
  17, 19, 72; biography of, 64–67;
  video/movie director, 21, 24,
  38, 74, 104
Peters, Duane, 20, 24, 30, 75;
  biography of, 67–68
Pezman, Steve, 17
Philadelphia, Pennsylvania,
  United States, 45
Phillips, Willie, 10
Phnom Penh, Cambodia, 2
Photography Exposure, 28, 59
Physical Education Classes,
  Skateboarding in, 35
Pier 7, 46
Pipe Utilization, 12, 16, 21
Plan B, 69, 78
Plexiglass Half Pipe, 67
Pokress, David, 32
Police Academy 4 (movie), 25
Polyurethane Wheels, 91
Ponce, Gaby, 41
Pool Skating, 12, 15, 21, 39, 91,
  95; events, 57
Port Alegre, Brazil, 82
Portland, Oregon, United States,
  38, 43, 77
Potential Energy, 97
Powell, George, 65
Powell Peralta (Company), 23, 36,
  63, 97
Powell Peralta Bones Brigade, 50
Pro/Am Skateboard Races
  Association, 19
Professional Skateboard
  Organizations, 19, 32–33, 37
Professional Status, 104

Pro-Tec Pool Party, 57
Public Sector, 106–107
Punk/Indie Bands, 24
Punk Rock, 67

Quarterly Skateboarder, 10, 17.
    See also Skateboarder
    (Magazine)
Queer as Folk (Television
    Show), 50
Quiksilver (Brand), 74, 104
Quiksilver Tony Hawk Show, 87

Racism, "White Sport," 51, 83
"Ramp It Up: Skateboard
    Culture in Native America"
    (Art Exhibit), 51
Ramp Skating, 12, 21. See also
    Vertical Skating
Ranking System, 33
Rawls, Louann, 72
Real (Company), 50
Rebellious Ethos, 20, 26, 30
Red Bull, 36
Red Hot Chili Peppers (Musical
    Group), 24, 72
Redondo Beach, California,
    United States, 67
Reebok, 38, 84
Reno, Nevada, United
    States, 54, 71
Reyes, Jamie, 85
Riding Giants (Movie), 66
Rio De Janeiro, Brazil, 82
Riordan, Bill, 18
Rising Sun (Movie), 104
Risk-Taking Ethos, 99, 101
Riverside, California, United
    States, 84

Rob and Big (Television Show), 2,
    37, 79
Rob Dyrdek Foundation, 35
Rob Dyrdek/DC Shoes Skate
    Plaza Foundation, 79
Rob Dyrdek's Fantasy Factory
    (Television Show), 2, 37, 47, 79
Rocco, Steve, 22–23, 25–27, 69
Rocket Air, 71
Rodriguez, Matt, 50
Rodriguez, Paul "Prod" Jr.,
    32, 79, 93
Roller-Skating, 19
Rolling Stone (Magazine), 44
Rowley, Geoff, 33, 57
Rules and Regulations, Skate
    Parks, 100
Rutland, Ohio, United States, 44
RVCA (Brand), 51, 104

S-K-A-T-E (game), 47–48, 56
Sablone, Alexis, 41
Sacramento Kings, 57
Salaries, Women Pay Increase, 40
Salba, 68
San Diego, California, United
    States, 15, 73, 77, 79, 85
San Francisco, California, United
    States, 4, 46, 50, 56, 68, 81; Bay
    Area, 52
San Francisco's Fisherman's
    Wharf, 100
Santa Barbara, California, United
    States, 63
Santa Cruz (Company), 25
Santa Cruz Skateboards, 18, 68
Santa Monica, California, United
    States, 16, 58, 61
Sao Paulo, Brazil, 82

Schafer, Brian, 54
Schmitt, Paul, 35, 93
Search for Animal Chin
(Video), 24
Segovia-Krause, Patty, 30, 39, 54,
101; biography of, 70–71
Semiao, Ron, 31
Senizergues, Pierre-Andre, 104
"Separation of Church and Skate"
(Song), 41
Sex in the City (Television
Show), 50
Shanghai, China, 39, 48
Shanghai Showdown, 48
Shaw Millennium Park, 48
Sheckler, Ryan, 7, 40, 79, 93
Shut Skates, 51
"Sidewalk Surfin' " (Song), 41
Signal Hill Speed Run, 15, 58
Simi Valley, California, United
States, 33
Simpson, Bart, 2
The Simpsons (Television
Show), 1
Sims (Company), 92
Singapore, 35
Six Flags, 75
"Skate and Create" Motto, 21
"Skate and Destroy" Motto, 20
"Skate and Destroy" (Song), 41
"Skate Betty," 22
Skate Lab, 33
Skate Moms
(Organization), 34, 39
Skate Park Association of the
United States, 35
Skate Park of Tampa (SPoT), 54
Skate Parks, Development, 12, 33,
35–36

Skate Pass, 2, 35
"Skate Town" (Song), 41
"Skateboard" (Song), 41
"Skateboard Anarchy"
(Song), 41
Skateboard (Movie), 18
Skateboard, Parts of a, 91
"Skateboard Boy" (Painting), 19
Skateboard Hall of Fame, 33
Skateboard Innovations, 12, 13
Skateboard Madness
(Movie), 17, 65
Skateboarder (Magazine),
12, 17, 61
Skateboarding Ethos, 1, 3, 21, 25,
31, 34, 40, 68, 101; role of
media, 29–30
Skateboarding-Themed Art, 104
Skateboarding Turkey, 37
Skateboardmania (Movie), 18
Skateboardmania (Theatrical
Production), 68
Skateboard.TV, 83
Skateistan, 2
"Sk8ter Boi" (Song), 2, 41
Skater Girls (Reality Television
Show), 37, 71
Skaterdater (Movie), 11
Skatergirl, 39
Skatespot Liberation Front, 100
Skatopia, 44
Skatopia: 88 Acres of Anarchy
(Movie), 44
Skirtboarders, 38
"Skurban" Style, 38
Slalom Skateboarding, 15, 21
Slam (Novel by Nick Hornby), 38
Slam City Jam, 81, 82
Slap (Magazine), 27

SMAK (Stedelijk Museum voor Actuele Kunst), 49

Smith, Rodney, 51

Smithsonian National Museum of the American Indian, 51

SMP (Skate Park), 48

Snowboarding, 36, 52, 76

Social Distortion (Musical Group), 24, 70

Social Environment, 99

Social Media, 100

Social Networks, 101

Song, Daewon, 33, 69

Songs Dedicated to Skateboarding, 41

SONY Pictures Digital Entertainment, 32

Soul Artists of Zoo York, 50

Soul Bowl, 58

Soul Food Taqueria (Musical Album), 50

Sources of Income, 23

South Africa, 39

South Gate, 70

Speed, 92, 93, 94

Spinner, 15

Spitfire, 50

Sponsorships, 23, 32, 53, 59

St. Pius X High School, 70

Stability, 94

Stalefish, 73

Steamer, Elissa, 33, 85; biography of, 80–81

Stecyk, Craig, 17, 21, 24, 65, 104

Stern, Jeffery, 36

Stereotypes, 3; rebellious teenager, 9

Stevenson, Larry, 9

Steve's South Bay Contest, 67

Street Dreams (Movie), 79

The Street League, 40, 57, 79, 103

Street Luge, 15

Street Skating Events, 56

Street Style, 19, 46; becoming dominant style, 33

Strength (Magazine), 27

The Stupids (Musical Group), 41

Suicidal Tendencies (Musical Group), 24, 41, 70

Summer X Games, 56

Super Session (Movie), 17

Surf Crazy (Movie), 10

Surf Guide (Magazine), 9, 62

Surfer (Magazine), 17

Surfing, 9

Sustainability, 106

Swank, Tod, 26

Tail Design, 92

Tail Wheelie, 15

Tampa Am, 54

Tampa Pro, 54

Tehachapi, California, United States, 52

Templeton, Ed, 26, 30, 49, 51, 104

Ternasky, Mike, 69, 78

Tha Hood Games, 51

Tha Hood Games: Kids, Community and Comrades (Art Exhibit), 52

Thai L Stix, 67

Thames River, 48

Thiebaud, Jim, 50

Thornhill, Laura, 18; biography of, 66–67

Thrasher (Magazine), 20, 21, 23, 27, 66, 76, 77, 81, 82, 84

Thrashin' (1986), 25

Tignes, France, 55
Tokyo, Japan, 48
The Tonight Show (Television Show), 62
Tony Hawk Foundation, 35, 36
Tony Hawk, Inc., 74
Tony Hawk Pro Skater (Videogame), 74
Tony Hawk Skateboarding Underground 2, 44
Tony Hawk's Big Spin, 75
Tony Hawk's BoomBoom HuckJam, 49, 74
Tony Hawk's Demolition Show, 75
Tony Hawk's Videogame Series, 38, 44, 54
Topanga Beach, California, United States, 62
Torres, Veronica, 41; biography of, 84–85
Toy Machine (Company), 26, 50, 80
Traces, 49
Tracker (Brand), 25
Traction, 92
Trafton, George, 9
Transitions Art Gallery, 54
Transworld Skateboarding (Magazine), 20, 23, 27, 76
Treece, Chuck, 50
Trucks, 91
Tum Yeto (Company), 26
Turner, Laurie, 11
Turner, Vince, 10

United Kingdom Skateboarding Association, 37

United Professional Skateboarders Association, 40, 63
United Skate Front, 20
The United States Skateboard Association, 19
University of California, Davis, 75
University of California, Santa Barbara, 71
Upland Pipeline, 47, 57
The Uprising (Television Show), 73
Urban-Punk Style, 19, 21
Urethane (Wheels), 12
U.S. Bombs (Musical Group), 68
USA Skateboarding, 63

Val's Surf Shop, 10
Van Sant, Gus, 38, 44
Van Stone (Musical Group), 41
Vancouver, British Columbia, Canada, 81, 82
Vans (Company), 33, 38, 46, 49, 104
Vans Skatepark, 57
Vans Triple Crown, 76
Vapors (Magazine), 27
Vertical Skating, 21; becoming signature event of X Games, 31
Vickers, Vickie, 18
Video Days (Movie), 99
Video Exposure and Promotion, 23, 59, 97, 98
Videogames, 38, 105
Villa, Hailey, 62
Vision (Company), 24, 26
Vita-Pakt Juice Company, 10
Vitello, Fausto, 20, 21, 66
Viva La Bam (Television Show), 2

Warped Tour, 30, 49, 71; All Girl
   Skate Jam (AGSJ) inclusion, 55
Washington, DC, 51
Washington (State), 58
Wasssup Rockers (Movie), 38
Watson, Karl, 52
Way, Damon, 77
Way, Danny, 7, 8, 33, 40, 59, 71,
   93, 96; biography of, 77–78
Way, Kari, 78
Way, Mary, 77
Way, Rumi, 77
Way, Ryden, 77
Way, Tavin, 77
Welcome to Hell (Video), 80
Welinder, Per, 26
Wheels (of the Skateboard), 91
White, Shaun, 63
Wild Grinders, 79
Williams, Keith, 51
Williams, Stevie, biography of,
   83–84
Winkle, Willie, 92
Winston-Salem, North Carolina,
   United States, 64
Winter X Games, 55
Woman's Sports
   Foundation, 87
Women in Skateboarding. *See*
   Female Equity Issues
Women's Sport
   Foundation, 40

Woodward Camps, 3, 52, 104;
   history of, 52
World Anti-Doping Agency
   (WADA), 36
World Cup Skateboarding (WCS),
   33, 36, 76, 81, 82, 103
World Industries, 22, 23, 27, 69

X Games (Formerly Extreme
   Games), 3, 30, 31, 36, 39, 45;
   Global X, 55; history of, 55;
   influence on skateboarding, 37,
   40, 104; lack of diversity in, 52,
   73, 74, 81, 82, 84; Winter X
   Games, 55
X Games Asia, 39, 48
X Games Global
   Championships, 39

Youth Popular Culture, 3, 24, 30
Youth-Targeted Marketing, 3, 31

Z-Boys, 14, 24; formation
   of the, 65
Zephyr (Company), 14, 16, 17, 65
Zephyr (Skateboarder), 50
Zero, 81
'Zines, 30, 51
Zoo York, 50, 51
Zoo York Skateboard
   Company, 51
ZooBamboo Entertainment, 83

about the author

BECKY BEAL, EdD, is a Professor of Kinesiology at California State University–East Bay in Hayward, California, where she teaches courses in the sociology and philosophy of sport and serves as the Associate Director of the Center for Sport and Social Justice. Dr. Beal has been actively involved in the North American Society for the Sociology of Sport and served on the editorial board for the *Sociology of Sport Journal*. Beal has been researching the cultural and political dynamics of skateboarding for 20 years and has published 14 articles and book chapters on this topic. Her current work explores the relationship between "action" or "extreme" sports and other popular culture industries.